FACTS AT YOUR FINGERTIPS

ENDANGERED ANIMALS
MAMMALS OF THE NORTHERN HEMISPHERE

BROWN
BEAR
BOOKS

Published by Brown Bear Books Limited

4877 N. Circulo Bujia
Tucson, AZ 85718
USA

and

First Floor
9-17 St. Albans Place
London N1 ONX
UK

Library of Congress Cataloging-in-Publication Data

Mammals of the Northern Hemisphere / edited by Tim Harris.
    p. cm. – (Facts at your fingertips. endangered animals)
  Includes bibliographical references and index.
  Summary: "Describes various mammals in the Northern
Hemisphere that are endangered and at risk of becoming extinct.
Data Sheet sidebars and maps accompany the text"–Provided by
publisher.
  ISBN 978-1-936333-34-9 (library binding)
1. Rare mammals–Northern Hemisphere–Juvenile literature. 2.
Endangered species–Juvenile literature. I. Harris, Tim. II. Title. III.
Series.

QL706.8.M26 2012
599.16809181'3-dc22

2010053969

ISBN-13 978-1-936333-34-9

Editorial Director: Lindsey Lowe
Editor: Tim Harris
Creative Director: Jeni Child
Designer: Lynne Lennon
Children's Publisher: Anne O'Daly
Production Director: Alastair Gourlay

Printed in the United States of America

In this book you will see the following key at top left of each entry. The key shows the level of threat faced by each animal, as judged by the International Union for the Conservation of Nature (IUCN).

EX	Extinct
EW	Extinct in the Wild
CR	Critically Endangered
EN	Endangered
VU	Vulnerable
NT	Near Threatened
LC	Least Concern
O	Other (this includes Data Deficient and Not Evaluated)

For a few animals that have not been evaluated since 2001, the old status of Lower Risk still applies and this is shown by the letters **LR** on the key.

For more information on Categories of Threat, see pp. 54–57.

Picture Credits

Abbreviations: c=center; t=top; l=left; r=right.

Cover Images
Front: *Gray wolf*, Shutterstock/Nik Nikiz
Back: *Polar bear*, Thinkstock/Istockphoto

AL: Francois Gohier 36-37, Chris Harvey 5, Edwin Mickleburgh 61, M. Watson 34–35; **Anthony E. Cooper:** 20–21; **BCC:** Erwin and Peggy Bauer 23, Pete Oxford 49–50, Anup Shah 11, Vadim Sidorovich, Lynn M. Stone 17; **FLPA:** T. Andrewartha 24–25, Michael Callan 18–19, H. Clark 6t; F. Di Dominico/Panda 41; **IUCN:** 59; **NHPA:** Manfred Daneggar 30–31, Martin Harvey 12–13; **PEP:** Dr. Robert Franz 33; **Photolibary Group:** Marty Cordano 56, Tui De Roy 58, Nick Gordon 15, Howard Hall 6b, Mike Hill 48–49, Su Keren 27, Stan Osolinski 54–55, William Paton/Survival Anglia 44–45, Nobert Rosing 58–59, Vivek R. Sinka 8–9, Gerard Soury 42–43, Tom Ulrich 39, 47; **Thinkstock:** Stockbyte 57

Artwork © Brown Bear Books Ltd

Brown Bear Books has made every attempt to contact the copyright holder. If you have any information please email smortimer@brownbearbooks.co.uk

CONTENTS

What is a Mammal?

Mammals typically have a high body temperature, usually about 95 to 100°F (35 to 38°C). They are homeothermic, meaning that this temperature is normally kept fairly constant throughout the animal's life. Mammals are also referred to as endotherms, meaning that the warmth is generated internally, making them largely independent of external sources of heat such as the warmth of the sun. Their offspring are born as active babies and fed on milk secreted by the mammary glands of the mother. Echidnas and the platypus are exceptional in producing eggs, but still nourishing their young with milk.

Parental care, which sometimes lasts for years, is normal among mammals and allows the offspring to learn from older animals. Generally, families are small, and the young are well looked after to achieve a higher survival rate. Many species also live in social groups in which individuals cooperate to raise their young more successfully. Most mammals have a hairy or furry coat, which helps insulate them and maintain their high body temperature. Some—whales, for example—are nearly hairless as an adaptation to their particular way of life, but insulation is then provided by large amounts of fat (blubber) under the skin. In conjunction with their warm body mammals also have a very efficient blood circulatory system. It works faster and at higher pressures than in all other animals except birds. Endothermic homeothermy (warm-bloodedness) and an efficient blood system enable muscles and nerves to work faster, speed up digestion of food, help babies grow more rapidly, and generally assist mammals in living a much more active life than most other creatures.

Variations on a Theme

The basic mammal body plan, including four feet each with five toes, has been modified to allow the development of highly efficient diggers, runners, swimmers, and fliers. The teeth are also specialized to cope with many different kinds of food, from meat to nuts, leaves, fish, grass, blood, and insects.

These characteristic features of mammals enable them to live in a wide variety of habitats more independently of their surroundings (air temperature, for example) than any other animals. Mammals occur on all the continents—in the polar regions, deserts, mountaintops, and jungles. Some can make prolonged dives into deep oceans. Mammals can survive successfully in a wider diversity of habitats than any other animal group of comparable size. One species (our own) has even left this world to visit another—no other animal ever did that!

Mammals and People

Some mammals have become very abundant and widespread. Many (such as horses, dogs, cattle, and sheep) have also played a key role in the success of our own species, helping humans in their conquest of the planet by providing us with meat, milk, leather, transportation, and muscle power. Some assist in medical research to aid our own species, but others are significant pests and carriers of disease.

The History of Mammals

The first mammals evolved when dinosaurs ruled the world, about 100 million years ago. Mammals are therefore a comparatively new group of animals; many others have a much more ancient origin. Reptiles, for example, first appeared over 200 million years earlier. The first mammals were small and insignificant creatures that looked like today's solenodons and gymnures. From simple beginnings mammals have evolved into a wide assortment of species based on shared features and now include the blue whale, the largest animal ever. The smallest mammal is the

The earliest mammals
were small, inconspicuous insect-eaters like the long-extinct Megazostrodon (above). Over the last 200 million years mammals have come to dominate the planet, and now the group includes animals as diverse as bats, kangaroos, sea otters (left), and humans.

Etruscan shrew; at about 2 grams it is smaller than many beetles. Over the last one to two million years enormous changes have taken place in the variety of mammal species present in different parts of the world. Many have become extinct or been reduced to critically small numbers.

Why Are Mammals at Risk?

In historic times mammals have suffered heavily from attacks by humans, particularly the larger and fiercer species (such as the tiger, pp. 10–11, gray wolf, pp. 20–21, and polar bear, pp. 24–25) that were considered to be a threat to our own survival or a danger to domestic animals. Large mammals are also in danger simply because of their size. American bison (pp. 46–47), for example, take up a lot of space and need a great deal of food every day. A bison might eat the same amount as, say, two cows, but the same vegetation cannot feed both. The same patch of ground cannot grow grass for bison, while at the same time providing grazing for domesticated animals or producing crops for people. Around the world, the expansion of farmland has pushed wild animals back into less suitable areas, and their numbers have dwindled—in the example of the American bison, dramatically. In other parts of the world, the wild mammals (elephants, for example) have been forced to steal from the crops planted on the land they used to occupy. They are then called pests and eliminated with guns, traps, and poisons. Even using more humane forms of control, such as putting up fences instead of killing the animals, forces them to live in smaller areas that cannot support such high numbers. It is the larger species that have suffered most simply because they need large amounts of space, just as we do. Get rid of an elephant herd, and it creates room for 100 people and their crops. As numbers of humans have increased, wild mammals have been pushed aside. For example, during a 30-year period when elephants declined drastically in Kenya, the high human birthrate there meant that the lost elephants were replaced by almost exactly the same total tonnage of people. Domestic mammals such as cattle, sheep, and goats have everywhere increased in numbers, replacing their wild relatives and competing for the limited amounts of available food.

Exploitation

Some wild mammals have been specially hunted for their skins (such as the European mink, pp. 28–29), meat (for example, the wild yak, pp. 50–51), or other products. Overexploitation has led to catastrophic population declines. Again, this particularly affects the larger species because they do not breed rapidly, having few young and taking a long time to reach

The lifeless body *of a gray whale, washed up on a beach after it was ensnared in a discarded fishing net. Accidental deaths—ranging from roadkills to incidents such as this—claim the lives of mammals the world over.*

breeding age. Populations cannot cope with large numbers being killed, and they collapse. Larger mammals also tend to live longer, often more than 20 years. That allows time for poisons and other pollutants (such as heavy metals and polychlorinated biphenyls, known as PCBs) to accumulate and take effect, preventing breeding and causing sickness and sometimes even death. The accumulation of poisons is less of a problem for animals that naturally live for only a short time.

Some mammals (such as whales and many large land species) are thinly spread over a wide area. Their distribution therefore suggests a level of abundance that is misleading. They seem to be common, but widespread populations that are thin on the ground are vulnerable to fragmentation. Once the population is broken into small groups, they often include too few to be viable, and they die out one after another. Some

The lack of natural food sources *as a result of habitat disturbance can result in young being abandoned and conservationists intervening. Here bats are fed from a syringe on goats' milk.*

Percentage of mammals threatened
- 0–7
- 7–12
- 12–17
- 17–100

Northern hemisphere *countries that have the highest percentage of threatened mammals (above) include India, Ukraine, and Vietnam.*

species are at risk from interbreeding with their domesticated relatives, creating hybrids.

Smaller Species

Small mammals have problems too. Their size makes them vulnerable to predators and to cold weather. At least half of all known mammal species are rat-sized or smaller. One-third of all mammals are rodents (rats, mice, squirrels, and so on), and one in five is a bat. These animals are often difficult to study and are normally largely ignored. This means that we simply do not know what their real status is. Their numbers are unknown and not monitored. Many may go extinct them ever being recorded as being present.

These are special problems for mammals; but like other animals, the mammals also suffer from habitat destruction. Those that are adapted to a particular way of life suffer heavily from the cutting down of trees or the mass removal of their food (such as fish) to feed humans. This is a particular problem where populations are small to start with.

Numbers of Threatened Species in Each of the Major Mammalian Groups	
Rodents (mice, squirrels, and beavers)	461
Bats	253
Carnivores (dogs, cats, bears, and otters)	98
Primates (monkeys, apes, and lemurs)	224
Ungulates (horses, rhinos, hippos, deer, and antelope)	149
Marsupials	61

Rodents, *which constitute 30 percent of all mammals, represent the highest number of threatened species (above).*

The Situation Today

There are about 5,500 species of mammal (but nearly 10,000 species of birds and almost 40,000 fish). About 80 to 90 mammal species have become extinct in the last 300 years, and many subspecies and local varieties are also extinct or nearly so. Of the living species about 3.4 percent are now Critically Endangered, 8.2 percent Endangered, and 9.0 percent Vulnerable. In total about 25 percent of all known mammals are significantly threatened in some way. That is about twice the proportion of threatened birds. The most endangered major group is the primates: 45 percent of all primates are threatened.

Asiatic Lion

Panthera leo persica

The African lion may be familiar and still relatively numerous, but the Asian subspecies has become rare and is now confined to a single reserve in northwestern India.

Lions are widespread over much of Africa south of the Sahara, but one subspecies—the Barbary lion—used to occur only in the north. The Barbary was the animal seen in Roman arenas fighting gladiators to the death. At one time the Barbary lions and their close relatives were found from northern Africa throughout the Middle East to India. All are now extinct; but a similar subspecies, the Asiatic lion, survives in the Gir Forest in northwestern India.

A Shrinking Range

Because of the threat that lions pose to humans and livestock, they have been systematically eradicated from most of their former range. The last European lions were killed about 1,000 years ago; and once guns became widely available, they disappeared rapidly from the Middle East along with other large animals. In India British soldiers and Indian nobles hunted the Asian subspecies for sport. By 1900 only a few dozen were left; they lived in the Gir Forest, where a local prince protected them.

At that time the dry savanna and deciduous forest covered about 1,000 square miles (2,600 sq. km), but it has since shrunk to half that size. Much of what remains is now protected as a national park. The area is small, however, and is surrounded by cultivated land, so the lions are effectively marooned on a patch of suitable habitat of little more than 20 to 40 square miles (50 to 100 sq. km).

Moreover, they do not have the forest to themselves; there are several temples in the park, and five main roads and a railway track cross it. Large numbers of people are present at all times, and some have been killed by the lions; there were 81 attacks on humans, resulting in 16

DATA PANEL

Asiatic lion

Panthera leo persica

Family: Felidae

World population: About 360

Distribution: Gir Forest, Gujarat State, northwestern India

Habitat: Dry forest and acacia savanna

Size: Length head/body: up to about 6.5 ft (2 m); tail: about 3 ft (1 m). Weight: male 350–420 lb (160–190 kg); female 240–260 lb (110–120 kg)

Form: Similar to African lion, but with thicker coat and longer tail tassel; more pronounced tuft of hair on elbows; males do not develop large mane

Diet: Mainly deer and medium-sized mammals

Breeding: Average of 2 or 3 cubs per litter born after 4-month gestation. Young take 4–8 years to reach maturity. Life span up to about 20 years

Related endangered species: Tiger *(Panthera tigris)* EN; snow leopard *(Uncia uncia)* EN

Status: IUCN CR

PAKISTAN
NEPAL
BHUTAN
CHINA
INDIA
BANGLADESH
Gir Forest
SRI LANKA

Female Asiatic lions *rear their young together and suckle cubs other than their own for up to six months. The cubs start eating meat at three months.*

deaths between 1988 and 1990. To ease the problem, the sanctuary has been extended.

However, space is limited. Over 100,000 people live with their livestock within 6 miles (10 km) of the park. Domestic animals compete for food with the wild deer that the lions need as prey. When the lions go hungry, they turn to killing cattle. The government compensates local farmers for losses, but even so, lions are killed in revenge from time to time.

The cramped conditions create another danger. With the last Asiatic lions confined to one small area, there is a risk that the entire population could be wiped out by disease. In 1994 an outbreak of distemper left scores of African lions dead in Serengeti National Park in Tanzania, eastern Africa; a similar disaster in the Gir Forest could make the Asiatic lion extinct. One solution would be to establish another population elsewhere. One attempt to start a new population has already failed, probably as a result of illegal poisoning and shooting of the animals, but Kuno Wildlife Sanctuary in Madhya Pradesh, India, has been proposed as a new reintroduction site.

Tiger

Panthera tigris

Tigers used to occur across Asia as far west as Turkey, and isolated populations developed into eight different subspecies.

The tiger *is the largest member of the cat family. There are thought to be about 4,500 in India, the species' main stronghold.*

Within their huge range tigers have adapted to conditions ranging from bleak mountain forests to mangrove swamps and jungle. Since the beginning of the 20th century numbers have sharply declined, usually through conflict with humans. Tigers are large and fierce animals. They need to kill to eat and will often kill domestic animals and even people. Their own habitat has been reduced by farming and logging to the point where natural prey is difficult to obtain in sufficient quantity. Humans hunt the same prey, leaving few animals for the tigers.

By the 1950s three of the tiger subspecies (Bali, Caspian, and Javan) had become extinct. The remaining populations occur in widely separate places: India, Vietnam, Sumatra, China, and Siberia. The largest subspecies, the Amur (or Siberian) tiger, once ranged throughout the forested areas of China and Korea, north to the forested edges of Siberia. However, in the late 19th century tigers were a major threat to railway construction and increased settlement, so they were persecuted. By the 1940s tigers survived only in about five separated areas. Since then they have benefited from protection, and they have now increased in numbers and distribution again. There were about 450 Amur tigers in 1996. However, climate change now poses new threats.

On Bali and Java the extinction of the tiger was a result of habitat fragmentation, loss of natural prey, and finally, in the 1960s, conflict with groups of heavily armed men hiding in the jungle as a result of civil war. In India tigers used to be a favorite target for big-game hunters, and many thousands were shot.

Throughout Asia the tiger is believed to have magical powers, and many of its body parts are highly prized in traditional Oriental medicine. Killing a single tiger, therefore, can bring huge rewards to a poacher willing to risk the penalties for breaking the law.

Captive Breeding

Tigers breed well in captivity, so they are unlikely to become extinct. However, the captive population has become seriously inbred in the past, and there has been genetic mixing between the different subspecies. In addition, tigers cost a lot to feed, so most zoos give the animals contraceptives as a way of controlling the numbers of young born. It would be relatively easy to breed captive tigers for reintroduction to the wild, but there is not enough suitable habitat left for release of captive-bred stock.

The future lies in careful management of the remaining tiger habitats and reserves. Conservation measures will include linking small, isolated groups of animals and preventing poaching and further habitat loss. It is also vital to have plenty of prey animals; huge areas of land need to be set aside to maintain the prey populations required to support just a few tigers. The dangers of inbreeding may be reduced by using captive-bred animals as a fresh gene source.

DATA PANEL

Tiger

Panthera tigris

Family: Felidae

World population: 3,200–5,000 (2006 estimate)

Distribution: From India east to China and Vietnam and south to Indonesia (Sumatra)

Habitat: Dense cover: forests, scrub, and tall grass thickets; also mangroves

Size: Length head/body: 4.5–9 ft (1.4–2.7 m); tail: 24–43 in (60–110 cm); height at shoulder: 31–43 in (80–110 cm). Weight: up to 790 lb (360 kg) in the largest Siberian tigers

Form: Unmistakable, large orange cat with black stripes and long tail

Diet: Mostly deer and wild pigs weighing 110–440 lb (50–200 kg). Occasionally smaller animals such as monkeys, fish, and even birds. Needs about 33–40 lb (15–18 kg) per day

Breeding: Two or 3 cubs per litter, born after 14-week gestation; about 2 years between litters. Life span 15 years in wild, at least 26 in captivity

Related endangered species: Snow leopard *(Uncia uncia)* EN; lion *(Panthera leo)* VU; clouded leopard *(Neofelis nebulosa)* VU; also several smaller species of cat, including Iberian lynx *(Lynx pardinus)* CR

Status: IUCN EN

Clouded Leopard

Neofelis nebulosa

The clouded leopard gets its name from the cloudlike markings on its coat. The hunting of this big cat for its magnificent pelt is one of several threats to its survival.

The clouded leopard is not actually a leopard at all. In fact, the species is sufficiently distinct to be classified all by itself. The skull and teeth of the clouded leopard are similar to those of big cats such as lions and tigers. However, it is unable to roar loudly like its large cousins, and its appearance is more like that of smaller cats, including lynx and ocelots.

The Malaysian name for the clouded leopard is rinaudahan, meaning tree tiger, and it is indeed one of the most accomplished feline climbers. Its broad, flexible paws grasp branches, and its long tail serves as an effective counterbalance. The clouded leopard also has remarkably flexible ankle joints—captive individuals have been observed dangling upside down from branches by just one back leg! Its arboreal skill is put to good use when hunting; the leopard will sometimes ambush unsuspecting prey by pouncing on them from above. It captures and kills monkeys and birds by knocking them off the branches of trees, just as a domestic cat swipes at smaller prey. Nevertheless, this

adaptable cat also does much of its hunting on the ground, stalking wild pigs, deer, and cattle until it is close enough to launch a sudden fatal attack.

Starting Life

Little is known about the clouded leopard's social behavior and courtship in the wild, except that the animals appear to be solitary until the breeding season begins. Studies of individuals in zoos around the world have provided basic information about how the clouded leopard breeds. The young are born after a gestation of approximately three months. Each cub weighs 5 to 10 ounces (150 to 280 g) at birth, and its eyes remain closed for the first 10 to 12 days. The young begin to take solid food

DATA PANEL

Clouded leopard

Neofelis nebulosa

Family: Felidae

World population: Unknown, but no more than a few thousand

Distribution: Asia, including Nepal, southern China, Burma, Indochina, parts of India and possibly Bangladesh, mainland Malaysia, Sumatra, Borneo and Java, Thailand, Vietnam; probably now extinct in Taiwan

Habitat: Dense mountain forests

Size: Length head/body: 28–43 in (75–110 cm); tail: 35–59 in (90–150 cm). Weight: 25–66 lb (16–30 kg)

Form: Large, robust-looking cat with short legs and a long tail. The yellowish coat is distinctively marked with large dark patches, each with a pale, cloudlike center. The underside, legs, and head are spotted and streaked. The eyes are yellow, and the ears are rounded

Diet: Deer, cattle, goats, wild pigs, monkeys, reptiles, and birds; stalked or ambushed by day and night

Breeding: Only observed in captivity; 1–5 (usually 2–4) young born March–August. Lives up to 17 years in captivity

Related endangered species: No close relatives. Taiwanese subspecies may already be extinct

Status: IUCN VU

after 10 to 11 weeks, but the mother will continue to suckle them until they are about five months old. They are born with plenty of yellowish-gray fur marked with dark spots. The adult coat is developed at six months, and the youngsters reach independence about three months later.

A Fragile Future

There are four geographically distinct subspecies of clouded leopard, found in Taiwan, Borneo and Malaysia, Nepal and Burma, and also China. However, there have been no recent sightings of the Taiwanese subspecies, known as the Formosan clouded leopard, and there are fears that it may already have become extinct in the wild. Elsewhere the clouded leopard survives in the most remote and undisturbed areas of mountain forests. The main problems facing the

Clouded leopards *prefer to live in dense tropical forest, where they are found at altitudes of up to 7,000 feet (2,100 m). However, they will also occupy more marginal habitats such as swampy areas and sparsely forested terrain.*

animal throughout its range are all too familiar. It is hunted for its magnificent pelt, and its teeth and bones are considered prized ingredients in traditional Eastern medicines. Erosion of the clouded leopard's habitat—as a result of deforestation by the timber industry and forest clearance for human settlement—is even more of a problem. Even when they are not being persecuted, the leopards are running out of places to live. Clouded leopards are being bred in captivity around the world, so reintroduction programs may be possible in the future, but that can only happen if areas of suitable habitat can be preserved.

Iberian Lynx

Lynx pardinus

The Iberian lynx, once widespread in Spain and Portugal, may now be the world's most endangered cat. Although legally protected since the 1970s, it is still endangered as a result of habitat loss, persecution, and threats to its prey.

The Iberian lynx is smaller than the European lynx, but otherwise similar. Although previously widespread in Spain and Portugal, it is now a rare species. By the 1980s there were probably fewer than 1,200 lynxes alive. By 1999 the population had halved, and the distribution of the lynx had contracted by more than 80 percent in fewer than 30 years. Today there are probably fewer than 150 lynxes left. The main population lives in the mountains of central southern Spain. The rest are widely scattered, and all these subpopulations have a total of fewer than 100 animals. The Iberian lynx may be extinct in Portugal.

The Iberian lynxes live in open woodland with scattered pines and evergreen oaks. They also favor thick scrub, patches of open grassland, and dense thickets of dry scrub on the mountains. Rabbits comprise 80 percent of their diet, a degree of specialization that is dangerous in a changing world. To rely too much on one source of food makes any

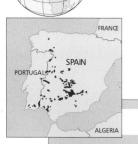

animal vulnerable if something goes wrong with the supply. In the 1950s the viral disease myxomatosis swept through the rabbit populations of Europe, killing over 90 percent of them in some places. As the years went by, the rabbit population became more resistant to this fatal disease, and numbers began to recover. However, in the late 1980s a new disaster struck in the form of rabbit hemorrhagic disease, which also killed large numbers of rabbits, again leaving few to support the lynx population.

Habitat Loss

The rapid economic development of Spain and Portugal over recent decades has been a significant threat to the lynx. Remote parts of the countryside have been opened up by the construction of new roads. Hotels and vacation homes have been built to accommodate the booming tourist industry and provide facilities for retirement communities. Overstocking of cattle and game ranches and the erection of deer fencing have also had a detrimental

DATA PANEL

Iberian lynx (pardel lynx)

Lynx pardinus

Family: Felidae

World population: 84–143

Distribution: Parts of Spain and Portugal

Habitat: Open pine woodland and among dense, dry thickets of scrub on the mountains

Size: Length head/body: 31.5 in–38 in (80–96 cm); tail: 3.5–4.5 in (9–11 cm); height at shoulder: 24–27 in (60–68 cm). Weight: 22–33 lb (10–15 kg)

Form: A large, long-legged cat, with a short black-tipped tail and tufted ears. Coat pale brown with white spots

Diet: Mainly rabbits, but also young deer, rodents, and ground-dwelling birds

Breeding: Breeding season January–March, births in May. Litters of 2–3 kittens born; 1 litter per year. Life span unknown, but other lynx species live up to 15 years

Related endangered species: Cheetah (*Acinonyx jubatus*) VU; tiger (*Panthera tigris*) EN; snow leopard (*Uncia uncia*) EN; several other big and small cats

Status: IUCN CR

The Iberian lynx *has an attractive gray-brown mottled coat, a broad, short head, and distinctive tufted ears. It is now one of the world's rarest mammals.*

effect on the habitat for many forms of wildlife, including the lynx. The natural mosaic of habitats that suits lynxes and their prey has been broken up, and the lynx population has been reduced and critically fragmented into nine separate subpopulations, with a total of at least 48 separate breeding groups. Increased use of roads has meant more deaths, particularly in the Coto Doñana area, and some populations of lynx already have fewer than 10 females, so even a few road kills per year could be disastrous.

Persecution

Although lynxes have been legally protected in Spain since 1973 and Portugal since 1974, many are still shot. Most live on private estates and cattle ranches, where hunting and shooting are common. Only 40 to 50 lynxes live in the protected area of the Coto Doñana National Park; very few enjoy the protection of nature reserves. Lynxes have now been infected with tuberculosis (TB) from wild pigs and deer.

Action Plan

An action plan for the lynx now exists: The European Habitats Directive has given the species more protection, and there should be money available from the European Union to manage the countryside in a manner more suited to wildlife conservation. However, it may all have come too late to save the Iberian lynx.

Florida Panther

Puma concolor coryi

The last few individuals of the once-widespread Florida panther cling precariously to their remaining habitat in the southern United States. This handsome cat now faces possible extinction.

Like the ocelot, the panther (or puma) has a very wide distribution throughout North and South America. There are various local subspecies, one of which is the Florida panther. The panther has been extinct in Arkansas, Louisiana, Tennessee, and West Virginia since the 1950s. Another subspecies, the eastern panther, has probably also died out, leaving only the Florida panther in the eastern United States.

Almost everything that has happened to its environment in the last 100 years has hit the panther hard. It is a familiar story: As the human population has expanded and increased its activities, so panthers have been eliminated. They are large predators, presenting a threat to both people and their livestock. Farm animals have been attacked, and on average one person a year is killed by panthers in North America. These few attacks may not seem significant, but they give the animals a bad public image, cause widespread fear, and result in a desire to eliminate them. Consequently, in many states hunters have been employed to kill panthers.

However, the main cause of the panther losses in Florida is change to its habitat. The creation of new farmland areas from the dense bush and palmetto (small palm) thickets has deprived the panthers of living space. New highways slice through the remaining habitat, creating areas too small to support a viable population. Young panthers normally disperse between 18 and 50 miles (30 to 80 km) from where they were born, but then the fast-moving traffic on the roads poses a danger. Roads and other barriers prevent animals from mixing and meeting, and there is then more inbreeding and consequently a loss of genetic diversity. The species then faces the threat of breeding failure, including a higher proportion of birth defects and miscarriages.

Much of Florida lies on limestone overlaid by swamps. In recent times 40 percent of the swamplands have been lost as a result of expansion of farmland. Water is pumped from underground to

DATA PANEL

Florida panther

Puma concolor coryi

Family: Felidae

World population: Between 70 and 80

Distribution: South central Florida

Habitat: Swamp forest and dense thickets

Size: Length head/body: 42–54 in (100–130 cm); tail: 30–36 in (72–80 cm); height at shoulder: 26–31 in (62–75 cm). Weight: 66–125 lb (30–57 kg)

Form: Large, tawny or dark-brown cat with white flecks around the shoulders; long black-tipped tail, sharply kinked toward the end. Black on sides of face and backs of ears

Diet: Deer; also hares, rodents, armadillos; occasionally domestic animals

Breeding: One to 6 (usually 3) cubs born at almost any time of year after gestation period of about 3 months; mature at 2–3 years. Life span about 20 years

Related endangered species: Eastern panther *(Puma concolor cougar)* CR

Status: IUCN CR

The Florida panther

population stands at fewer than 50 today, but the natural food supply available in Florida would once have supported about 1,300 panthers.

supply towns and irrigate crops. Swamps therefore dry up, and whole areas of forest and scrub become more susceptible to fire. Fire is devastating, not only because it kills wildlife, but also because it removes vital cover from large areas. The deer that form the main prey of the panthers are deprived of their food by the fires and also by the replacement of native vegetation by introduced plants (such as Brazilian pepper) that they do not eat, and the losses of deer affect the panther population.

In addition, panthers are at the end of a long food chain and therefore susceptible to the toxic materials that accumulate in their prey. Burning of domestic and industrial refuse in Florida gives out pollutants, which collect at every level of the food chain.

Chances of Survival

Legally protected since 1973, the Florida panther now survives only in and around the Everglades National Park and Big Cypress National Preserve. In 1995 eight females of the Texas subspecies were imported to provide fresh genes, and in 1980 a sperm bank was started to enable continued breeding of the animals. Major roads have now been fenced to reduce accidents with traffic, and habitat "corridors" are being created to allow safer movement. Nevertheless, the panther's future in Florida still looks bleak.

EX
EW
CR
EN
VU
NT
LC
O

Wildcat

Felis silvestris

Like many predators, the wildcat has suffered extensive persecution. Today the major threat to its survival is genetic dilution of the species as it increasingly interbreeds with domestic cats.

The wildcat is a solitary and secretive animal found mainly in forested areas across continental Europe and in Scotland. Its range also extends east to the Caspian Sea, an inland salt lake that lies between Europe and Asia. Its major prey is small mammals and birds: mostly mice, voles, rabbits, and other wild species. However, wildcats have been unpopular with humans, who suspect them of being a threat to domestic stock such as lambs and chickens and a danger to children. Although these fears are greatly exaggerated, the wildcat has been trapped, shot, and poisoned widely. Moreover, in the past its skin was prized for its warmth, and its fur became a luxury fashion item for trimming clothing.

Habitat Loss

The wildcat is not seriously endangered. However, the expansion of cities and intensification of farming have resulted in habitat loss. Although some wildcats manage to live close to farms and on the edges of European towns, where they may even visit garbage dumps to feed, they have become more scarce. There are now large areas of Europe where they are extinct, and the remaining populations are widely separated.

DATA PANEL

Wildcat

Felis silvestris

Family: Felidae

World population: More than 50,000, but in widely separated subpopulations

Distribution: Europe, east to the Caspian Sea

Habitat: Forested areas

Size: Length head/body: 22–30 in (50–75 cm); tail: 12 in (30 cm); height at shoulder: 16 in (40 cm). Weight: 10–30 lb (4.5–13.5 kg)

Form: Resembles a domestic tabby cat, but is larger and has 7–11 bold stripes on its flanks. The tail is banded with several clear rings and the tip is blunt, not pointed as in domestic cats

Diet: Small mammals and young rabbits; birds; also frogs and insects

Breeding: One litter per year, up to 8 kittens (normally 3–4), born May–August. Life span up to 10 years

Related endangered species: Iberian lynx *(Lynx pardinus)* CR; Iriomote cat *(Prionailurus bengalensis iriomotensis)* EN; various big cats

Status: IUCN LC

The wildcat *looks like a domestic tabby, but is larger and has more distinct body stripes and a blunt end to the tail.*

Interbreeding Problems

The biggest threat by far to wildcats is "genetic pollution" through interbreeding with domestic cats. The wildcats of Europe are so similar to the African wildcat (from which the domestic form is thought to originate) that some zoologists think the two species are actually the same. They are certainly closely related, which is why they interbreed so easily. As a result, the natural wildcat population has begun to include crossbred animals (hybrids). This genetic dilution undermines the purity of the species. Ironically, as the wildcat's habitat has shrunk, the animal has been forced into new areas where it encounters domestic cats more often. This has led to more interbreeding and further genetic dilution. Thus the greater the wildcat's breeding success, the more uncertain its future. At the very least, hybridization will result in a confused picture, with some areas having true wildcats, and others having hybrids. In addition, interbreeding makes the species difficult to monitor.

The Berne Convention, the European Union Habitats Directive, and the national legislation of many countries recognize the wildcat's rarity and have given the animal legal protection. Yet these laws are unable to prevent the main threat of interbreeding. Moreover, since hybrids are not legally protected, the legislation is weakened because anyone killing a wildcat can claim that they thought the animal was a hybrid. Such an assertion cannot be easily disproved. If wildcats and domestic cats really are the same species then it seems impractical to give the animal legal protection, since there are millions of house cats all over the world!

Gray Wolf

Canis lupus spp.

Although still common in Alaska and some other areas, the gray wolf is now extinct or critically endangered in many parts of its former range.

The gray wolf is the largest member of the dog family. At one time it had the widest distribution of almost any land mammal, being found nearly everywhere in the Northern Hemisphere. Throughout this range wolves have inspired considerable fear over the centuries, and this has been reinforced by spine-chilling stories; they are the subject of much folklore. As people and their domestic animals have spread and increased in number, conflict with wolves has escalated, resulting in extermination of wolves in many parts of their range.

Today there are thought to be 52,000–60,000 gray wolves in Canada and up to 9,000 in the United States. About 2,000 gray wolves still survive in Spain, and that number is growing. Also increasing is the Swedish population, and there are some wolves in southeast Norway (where the population is protected and farmers are paid compensation for livestock losses). Between 1991 and 1992 wolves spread from Italy as far as the French Alps, but at least six were shot soon afterward.

Today wolves are still unwelcome residents across much of their European range. In Romania there is a population of about 2,500 (though some are still shot). In Greece wolves face a shortage of suitable large mammal prey, but there is a stable population of 200–300 animals. In Italy, however, where farmers are paid compensation for sheep killed by wolves, local wolf populations seem to have increased a little, to about 700–800.

Fortunately, the wolf remains fairly abundant in northern territories particularly Alaska, Canada, and the former Soviet Union. There have also been attempts to reintroduce the animals to areas in which they had previously been eradicated. In 1995 wolves were released back into Yellowstone National Park in the United States, a move that was highly controversial.

DATA PANEL

Gray wolf (timber wolf)

Canis lupus spp.

Family: Canidae

World population: Many thousands (more than 50,000 in former Soviet Union and adjacent countries, for example, and more than 60,000 in North America)

Distribution: Canada and Alaska; also northern Asia and into Eastern Europe. Remnant populations in Spain, Portugal, Sweden, and Arabia

Habitat: Open woodland (especially coniferous forest), mountains, tundra, and bogs

Size: Length head/body: 39–51 in (100–130 cm); tail: 14–20 in (35–52 cm); height at shoulder: 26–28 in (65–70 cm). Weight: male 66–175 lb (30–80 kg); female 50–120 lb (23–55 kg)

Form: Large dog, almost white in northern latitudes; dark gray to nearly black farther south. Tail held high when running

Diet: Birds and small- to medium-sized animals; packs cooperate to kill larger species such as deer

Breeding: Between 3 and 7 cubs born per year in single litter after 9-week gestation; mature at 2 years (but often longer before they actually breed). Life span up to 20 years in captivity; probably 10–15 in wild

Related endangered species: Red wolf (*Canis rufus*) CR; Ethiopian wolf (*C. simensis*) EN; African wild dog (*Lycaon pictus*) EN; maned wolf (*Chrysocyon brachyurus*) NT

Status: IUCN LC

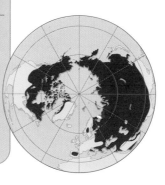

The fear of wolves runs deep, and there are concerns for the safety of cattle and sheep in the vicinity. Such projects can only succeed with public support; otherwise the animals are exterminated before a new population has time to establish itself.

A Shortage of Suitable Prey

A serious problem for wolves in Europe and in the more densely inhabited parts of North America is that the expansion of farming has reduced the numbers of deer and other suitable prey. Without sufficient food to support them, wolf populations have fragmented. Wolves have then been forced to attack sheep and to scavenge around garbage dumps, bringing them into more frequent contact with people and increasing the risk of crossbreeding with domestic dogs. In Spain a recent increase in the deer population was followed by

a reduction in the number of sheep killed by wolves. Since the wolves were preying on the deer, they did not need to kill the sheep. This small victory is a reminder that conservation initiatives need to look at the health of the environment as a whole as well as the fate of individual species.

Perhaps there is also encouragement to be gained from Canada, where wolf-watching trips are becoming popular activities in national parks. Growing familiarity may help reduce some of the fear that people have for the wild ancestor of the domestic dog, helping make the gray wolf's long-term future a little more secure.

Gray wolves *do not attack humans, despite the legends. People are at greater risk of dying from domestic dog attacks than from wolf attacks. Wolves do attack coyotes, however, and may help keep coyote numbers in check.*

Swift Fox

Vulpes velox

The small swift fox has suffered heavy losses as a result of trapping and poisoning campaigns intended to eradicate other more abundant carnivores that were thought to be a threat to livestock.

The swift fox is sometimes regarded as a North American subspecies of the common kit fox. However, the two have a different distribution, and the distinctive DNA and skeletal structures of the swift fox justify treating it as a separate species.

Swift foxes live in small family groups, occupying underground dens with an extensive system of burrows and chambers. The tunnels provide cool shelter during the heat of the day and hiding places in open habitats. For these reasons the burrows are also attractive to rodents and other small animals such as lizards and beetles, which also occupy the dens, providing the foxes with some extra food.

Threats to Survival

Swift foxes are found in open prairie and desert habitats. They used to occur from Canada in the north to the Mexican border in the south. However, in the more northerly states much of their habitat has been taken over as farmland. Swift foxes are relatively tame, and this has contributed to their decline. They are easily trapped, and many were caught for their fur; others have been shot or killed by road traffic. Swift foxes also fall prey to the coyote, a larger relative that is the main predator of the swift foxes' cubs.

Swift foxes are nocturnal hunters. They feed mainly on rabbits and small mammals, and in so doing probably help farmers by destroying pests such as rats and mice. In addition, they do not harm chickens or other livestock. Despite this, the severe decline of swift fox numbers has been caused by their becoming unwitting victims of poisoning campaigns. Poisons directed at coyotes and other predators that are more abundant and perceived as a threat to farm livestock

have been picked up by the foxes. In many areas state and local governments have actively encouraged large-scale poisoning campaigns aimed at reducing the numbers of coyotes. As a result, swift foxes became extinct in Canada and are now also very rare in the northern United States.

Reintroduction into Canada

Attempts to reintroduce the swift fox into Canada began in the early 1980s. From 1983 to 1997 a total of 91 wild foxes were caught and taken to Canada for release. They were joined by 841 more that had been raised in captivity. Seventeen sites were selected for the release of foxes in Alberta and south-central Saskatchewan. Initially the foxes were studied carefully after release and were provided with shelters, but after 1987 they were simply turned loose. The captive-bred animals seemed to cope well with freedom, even though most had never been outside a cage.

In 1988 more than 30 pups were reared in the wild, and a small population has become established in Alberta and Saskatchewan in Canada, and Montana in the United States. By 2001 the total Canadian population had risen to almost 900. The project has been criticized, since none of the animals were of Canadian stock, all coming from farther south. Moreover, swift foxes seem to have been slowly spreading northward on their own, suggesting that there was no need for human intervention. There are plans for further reintroductions in the United States.

The swift fox *is similar in appearance to the common red fox, but is much smaller. Along with the kit fox, it is the smallest member of the dog family in North America.*

DATA PANEL

Swift fox

Vulpes velox

Family: Canidae

World population: Low thousands

Distribution: Confined to western U.S.; was extinct in Canada but has been reintroduced

Habitat: Open plains and deserts

Size: Length head/body: 15–20 in (36–48 cm); tail: 9–12 in (22–30 cm). Weight: 4–6 lb (1.8–2.7 kg)

Form: Small, large-eared, buff-yellow fox with black markings on either side of muzzle and bushy tail with black tip

Diet: Small mammals; occasionally large insects

Breeding: Between 4 and 7 pups born February–April. Life span up to 7 years in the wild, 20 years in captivity

Related endangered species: Falkland Island wolf *(Dusicyon australis)* EX; red wolf *(Canis rufus)* CR; Ethiopian wolf *(C. simensis)* EN; African wild dog *(Lycaon pictus)* EN; bushdog *(Speothos venaticus)* NT; dhole *(Cuon alpinus)* EN

Status: IUCN LC

Polar Bear

Ursus maritimus

The polar bear is instantly recognizable by its white coat and huge bulk. Today the population is relatively stable.

This magnificent creature is the world's largest land-dwelling carnivore and evolved from the same common ancestor as the brown bear. The most striking feature of a polar bear is undoubtedly its thick coat. The hairs are virtually colorless; they lack any pigment, but tiny bubbles within the hairs create the impression of whiteness. There are two layers to the fur; a fleecy undercoat and an outer layer of longer guard hairs. The long hairs are hollow; they trap air inside their shafts, which provides insulation and helps keep the bear afloat when it is swimming.

Giant Hunters

White is the perfect color for an Arctic predator. There is little or no cover to conceal the animal from its prey, and it would be impossible for a polar bear to surprise an alert, intelligent creature like a seal were it not for its excellent camouflage. The bear's black nose can give it away however, and there are stories of polar bears stalking seals while trying to cover their noses with a paw! Polar bears have excellent eyesight and a superb sense of smell. They can detect young ringed seals hidden in dens in the ice and use their massive, muscular forelegs to dig them out for an easy meal.

The polar bear lives at the edge of the ice, where floes break away leaving cracks and channels of water. They are just as at home in the water as on land. Their big flat feet make efficient paddles: They swim well and are accomplished divers, able to stay underwater for up to two minutes at depths of 15 feet (4.5 m). They can leap from the water on to an ice floe over 6.5 feet (2 m) tall.

True nomads, polar bears often hitch a ride on a drifting ice floe, traveling many miles at a time. They will occasionally dig a den in the snow to rest or wait out severe weather. Most of the time they are solitary creatures, but their vast ranges overlap, so from time to time they encounter other bears. They do not fight over territory, but scraps over food are common, and females with young are very aggressive.

Most polar bears remain active throughout the year, even in the prolonged twilight of the Arctic winter. Pregnant females hibernate in dens dug into the snow. During this time a female's body temperature is reduced by as much as 13°F (7°C), and her heart rate can fall as low as eight beats a minute, just enough to stay alive.

The young polar bears are born in midwinter, while the mother is in hibernation. Weighing only 24 to 28 ounces (600 to 700 g) at birth, they spend the next three months suckling rich, fatty milk from the still-sleeping mother—by March they can weigh as much as 33 pounds (15 kg). This puts a huge strain on the mother's body, and by the spring she will have lost up to 40 percent of her body weight.

Young bears stay with their mother for up to two and a half years, during which time she will teach

them to swim, to hunt, and build snow dens. She will not breed while she is nursing; and when the time comes for her to mate, she will drive her cubs away. The adolescent cubs may stick together for a while, but soon go their separate ways.

Polar bears were always scarce, and they suffered from severe, uncontrolled hunting during the 20th century. "International" animals, they wander widely across the Arctic wastes, where they face no real barriers, traveling from one nation's part of the Arctic to another. Until the 1960s, when the five polar bear nations (Russia, Canada, Norway, Greenland, and the

The polar bear *is the largest carnivore on land. It may cover a range of over 100,000 square miles (260,000 sq. km) in its lifetime.*

United States) signed a conservation treaty, it was difficult to protect them or to research population size. Since then numbers have increased, and today's population seems stable, with most of the bears living in northern Canada. Controlled hunting is allowed in certain places, and the bears are also an important tourist attraction.

Giant Panda

Ailuropoda melanoleuca

Adopted as the emblem of the Worldwide Fund for Nature and popular the world over, the giant panda has come to symbolize endangered animals and efforts to save them.

The giant panda, *with its stubby tail and distinctive black-and-white markings, has always been popular in zoos. Captive-breeding attempts have attracted media attention, and the species probably owes its survival to its high profile.*

The giant panda is probably one of the most distinctive and instantly recognizable animals in the world, yet probably fewer than 100 have ever been seen alive outside China. Traditionally, pandas were associated with magical properties. As a result, they have been killed for their skins and body parts. Many have also been caught accidentally in snares set for the valuable musk deer.

Pandas breed very slowly: Females are fertile for only two to three days in the year. The young take over a year to reach independence and do not breed until they are at least five years old.

The giant panda is found in cool, damp, mountain bamboo forests. An individual may spend most of its time within a single square mile of a valley or mountain ridge in which it must find all the food it needs. The animals are specialized feeders. Although they will eat roots and even mice, their main diet is bamboo. Since bamboo is not very nutritious, the panda needs a great deal of it and must spend 10 hours a day feeding. It has a bony extension of the wrist—a kind of thumb—that helps it grip bamboo shoots firmly.

By the time winter arrives, supplies of bamboo in the panda's territory are running out. As temperatures drop, the animals need even more food to maintain their body heat, so they move to lower altitudes in search of more abundant growth. Such a migration is possible only so long as the main areas of panda habitat are intact. However, at lower altitudes mountain forests have been carved up for farmland; logging has also destroyed much of the panda's forest habitat. Sichuan Province, the panda's main home, lost a third of its forest in the late 20th century, leaving the animals isolated in small, inaccessible patches. However, there are now more than 60 dedicated reserves, covering over 70 percent of suitable habitat. The animal is well protected under Chinese law.

Threats and Solutions

The contraction of bamboo habitat presents a serious threat to the giant panda. The situation is made worse by the bamboo's peculiar habit of flowering every so often and then dying, a phenomenon that appears to be on the increase as a result of long-term climate change. It takes several years for a new crop to grow. Periodically, the panda's main food supply simply dies out over large areas. In the 1970s, when three species of bamboo flowered at once and then died, over 100 pandas (more than a tenth of the entire population) are known to have starved to death.

Nowadays the population is fairly stable, although perilously small and fragmented. Attempts at captive breeding have had limited success. A few young have been born—18 at Chengdu Panda Research Institute in 2008, for example—but their survival rate is low and none has survived in the wild. Protection of the species' habitat appears to be the most effective way to save the giant panda from extinction.

DATA PANEL

Giant panda

Ailuropoda melanoleuca

Family: Ursidae (sometimes considered one of the Procyonidae, or assigned its own family, the Ailuridae)

World population: About 1,600

Distribution: Central provinces of China

Habitat: Mountain bamboo forests up to 12,800 ft (3,900 m) above sea level

Size: Length head/body: 4–5 ft (1.2–1.5 m); tail: about 5 in (12–13 cm); height at shoulder: about 24 in (60 cm). Weight: 165–350 lb (75–160 kg)

Form: Stocky, bearlike animal with creamy-white fur; black legs, shoulders, ears, eye patches, and nose

Diet: Mainly bamboo; also bulbs and other plant materials; occasionally fish and small animals

Breeding: Up to 3 young born at a time, but normally only 1 is reared successfully. Pandas take more than 5 years to reach maturity and may not breed every year. Life span in captivity up to 34 years, probably much less in the wild

Related endangered species: Lesser panda (*Ailurus fulgens*) EN

Status: IUCN EN

European Mink

Mustela lutreola

Once widespread in Europe, native mink populations are now in rapid decline. The animal's future is under threat both from humans and from the introduced American mink.

Like its American cousin, the European mink inhabits waterside habitats and is found along river banks and at the edges of lakes. It is mainly nocturnal, operating out of a burrow or natural den among tree roots. Some take over burrows made by water voles, but a mink can dig its own home if necessary. Mink are territorial and normally live alone: They tend to be well spaced out, with an average of only one mink per mile of river bank. They swim and dive well, aided by their partly webbed feet, and capture most of their food in the water. They also hunt on land, using their sense of smell to track down small rodents, frogs, and other prey.

Only a century ago the European mink was found across northern Europe and in parts of northern Asia. It has been extinct in most of western Europe for decades and is now also extinct in eastern European countries such as Lithuania, probably also in Finland and Poland. It remains widespread in Russia, where over 95 percent of the surviving populations live, but their distribution and exact status are uncertain.

Reasons for their decline include eager hunting and trapping for their valuable fur. Mink are easy to catch, so the temptation to overharvest them has not been resisted, and their slow breeding rate has been unable to compensate for heavy losses. Females produce up to seven young but only once a year and the survival rate is often low. Kittens are raised without help from the male and are independent at about 10 weeks. Some disperse 30 miles (50 km) or more, especially in winter, when it may be necessary to travel such distances to find unfrozen water.

Man-Made Hazards

Mink face other problems, including water pollution. They have also been affected by habitat loss, since many rivers have been dammed to provide electricity or modified to prevent floods and allow cultivation of land along their edges. Even in relatively undisturbed areas such as Belarus recent surveys show the mink has been declining.

DATA PANEL

European mink

Mustela lutreola

Family: Mustelidae

World population: 20,000–25,000

Distribution: Belarus, Estonia, France, Georgia, Latvia, Spain, and widely in Russia

Habitat: River banks near temperate grassland

Size: Length head/body: 12–18 in (30–45 cm); tail: 4.5–7.5 in (12–19 cm). Weight: 1.3–1.75 lb (550–800 g)

Form: Small mammal resembling a small, short-legged cat; dark, glossy, brown fur with white around muzzle

Diet: Rodents, including water voles and muskrats, small birds, and aquatic invertebrates such as crayfish and mollusks

Breeding: Breeding season February–March; 4–7 young born April–June; 1 litter a year. Life span 7–10 years

Related endangered species: Wolverine (*Gulo gulo*) LC; Colombian weasel (*Mustela felipei*) VU; pine marten (*Martes martes*) LC; giant otter (*Pteronura brasiliensis*) EN

Status: IUCN EN

In addition to this, in 1926 American mink were imported into Europe to be reared on fur farms. Many of them escaped and now compete directly with their smaller European cousin for food, dens, and living space. It is also said that male American mink can mate successfully with female European mink. However, although the babies begin to develop, they never survive. Since mink have only one litter a year, crossbreeding means that female European mink waste a whole year's reproductive effort.

It appears that the American species is a more successful survivor, and in under 75 years it has spread throughout Scandinavia, much of Britain, and the Netherlands. Other populations are also spreading rapidly in France, Spain, Italy, and Germany. In places where both species of mink occur together, the European mink seems to die out within five to 10 years.

In 1992 a special breeding program for the European mink was established with the aim of maintaining a viable population in captivity. In 1997 there were 64 individuals in 10 zoos. In the wild the decline continues at an alarming rate, and the native wild mink seems destined to become extinct in western Europe. Efforts are being made to establish populations on offshore islands, safe from the dangers on the mainland.

The European mink *is smaller than its American cousin. Only 2 to 3 percent of the remaining population live in Europe. This one has matted fur, having just left the water.*

Pine Marten

Martes martes

In the 19th century culling by gamekeepers eliminated the pine marten from many parts of its range. Today the animal is more widely tolerated, and numbers are rising.

The pine marten is a cat-sized member of the weasel family. Its shape and size vary considerably across its range. The largest specimens are found in Denmark and western Europe; smaller ones occur farther east.

Pine martens are mainly active at night and like to use hollow trees or cavities among rocks as dens in which to sleep, shelter, and raise their young. They are forest-dwelling animals that are well adapted to climbing and leaping among the trees, and are commonly found in conifer forests up to the treeline. However, they also like to feed in open grassy areas, where they hunt for voles and ground-nesting birds. In parts of Ireland and in Switzerland pine martens also feed extensively on ripe fruit in the fall.

There is a popular belief that pine martens prey on squirrels. Although they do occasionally take juveniles, they are not as agile in the branches as adult squirrels and therefore usually leave them alone. From time to time pine martens raid the nests of wild bees for honey or eat rabbits and lemmings—particularly if they are in plentiful supply.

Easily Trapped

The pine marten is a very flexible, adaptable, and successful animal, yet it has become extinct in many areas, particularly southern Britain. Pine martens were widespread there even as late as the 19th century. However, the increasing popularity of shooting gamebirds on estates led to large numbers of gamekeepers being employed. It was their job to exterminate all predators that might kill the gamebirds, and the pine marten was especially victimized, being easily trapped or attracted to poisoned baits. The pine martens were progressively eliminated from most English counties and from Wales, although a few scattered individuals may have survived, even into the late 20th century.

With legal protection and fewer gamekeepers, the pine marten has recolonized parts of Scotland and may also establish itself in northern England once again. Recovery has been assisted by large-scale planting of conifer forests for commercial timber production. The forests not only provide the preferred habitat for pine martens but also, in their early stages of growth, support huge numbers of voles, the pine martens' favorite food.

DATA PANEL

Pine marten

Martes martes

Family: Mustelidae

World population: Probably over 200,000

Distribution: Most of Europe, from Spain to western Siberia, but scarce in many places

Habitat: Temperate pine forests up to the treeline; dens made in hollow trees and cavities in rocks

Size: Length head/body: 14–22 in (36–56 cm); tail: 7–11 in (17–28 cm); height at shoulder: 6 in (15 cm); female at least 10–12% smaller than male. Weight: 1.1–4.5 lb (0.5–2.2 kg)

Form: A long, thin cat-sized animal, with chocolate-brown fur, a bushy tail, and creamy-orange throat patch

Diet: Small mammals, particularly voles, but also birds, insects, and even seashore animals; sometimes ripe fruit

Breeding: One litter a year; usually 3 (but up to 6) young in each; mature at 14 months. Life span about 10–15 years; maximum 18 in captivity

Related endangered species: European mink *(Mustela lutreola)* EN; various otters and other mustelids

Status: IUCN LC

Changing Attitudes

Gamekeepers today are better informed about the habits of pine martens and therefore more tolerant of them. On the European continent gamekeepers were less vigorous in their extermination of the animals, so the species has remained more numerous there. Major threats now facing pine martens include busy roads and predation by eagle owls; some farmers also poison or trap the animals to protect their chickens.

In the early part of the 20th century pine marten numbers were severely depleted by the fur industry. The animal's coat was highly prized, and many thousands of pine martens were killed every year to satisfy demand. In some places commercial harvesting continues, although in Russia there has been an 80 percent drop in numbers caught since the 1920s, when pine martens were more abundant, and their fur was considered to be the height of fashion.

The pine marten
is a tree-dwelling member of the weasel family. Pine martens have been hunted heavily for their fur. They were also killed as a result of gamekeepers' efforts to eliminate predators.

Black-footed Ferret

Mustela nigripes

Not long ago black-footed ferrets did not exist in the wild. The wiping out of prairie dog burrows in which the animals lodged started their decline. Today captive-bred stock are being reintroduced into the wild, and there are now three self-sustaining populations in the United States.

The black-footed ferret was probably never abundant. Nonetheless, it used to be found across a broad swathe of the American short grass prairies, from Texas to beyond the Canadian border. It commonly made its home in prairie dog colonies (called towns), taking over part of the tunnel system for its own use as predator in residence. The prairie dogs (burrowing rodents of the squirrel family) made up over 90 percent of the ferret's diet. A single ferret could survive on what it could catch in even quite a small town, but mothers raising families normally took up residence in larger colonies. Mice and other small prey caught outside the burrow at night added to the ferret's prairie dog diet.

Black-footed ferrets do not gather in groups. Instead, they spread themselves out, often living about 3.5 miles (6 km) apart; the low density of animals presumably prevented them from overexploiting their food resources. The ferrets were so dependent on prairie dogs for both food and lodging that when—in the 20th century—prairie dog towns were wiped out wholesale to make way for farmland, the ferrets suffered along with their prey. In Kansas, a former prairie dog stronghold, over 98 percent of the prairie dog population was eliminated in less than 100 years. By the middle of the 20th century the ferrets were feared extinct, although there were reported sightings of individuals from time to time. A small population was even discovered in South Dakota, but the group had apparently died out by 1974.

Back from the Brink

In 1981 a black-footed ferret was killed by dogs on a ranch in Wyoming. Subsequent investigations revealed that a substantial wild population, numbering at least 129 animals, had survived there. The group became the subject of intensive study, but the white-tailed

DATA PANEL

Black-footed ferret

Mustela nigripes

Family: Mustelidae

World population: About 1,000 in the wild and 300 in captivity

Distribution: Formerly grasslands of the American Midwest from Texas to the Canadian border; reintroduced into Montana, South Dakota, Arizona, and Wyoming

Habitat: Short-grass prairies; in prairie dog burrows

Size: Length head/body: 15–24 in (49–60 cm); tail: 5–6 in (10–14 cm). Weight: 32–39 oz (915–1,125 g)

Form: Sinuous, short-legged animal, about the size of a small cat; pale yellow in color; black legs, mask, and tail tip

Diet: Mostly small rodents, especially prairie dogs, caught inside the prairie dog burrow. Mice and other small prey caught outside at night

Breeding: One litter per year in March–April; usually 3–4 (but up to 6) young born; young stay with their mothers until early fall. Male offspring may disperse; females often stay near birth site. Life span at least 12 years

Related endangered species: Colombian weasel *(Mustela felipei)* EN; European mink *(M. lutreola)* EN; Indonesian mountain weasel *(M. lutreolina)* DD; black-striped weasel *(M. strigidorsa)* LC

Status: IUCN EN

prairie dogs on which the ferrets were feeding had suffered a population crash as a result of disease, and the ferrets themselves had been struck down by an outbreak of canine distemper. The last 18 ferrets were taken into captivity as an insurance against total extinction. By 1987 there were no black-footed ferrets left in the wild.

An Uncertain Outlook

In captivity the ferrets' numbers built up slowly, to over 300 by the end of 1991—enough for some to be reintroduced to the wild. Since then more than 2,000 have been released at 18 locations, and in 2008 there were about 500 breeding adults in the wild. In the United States there are self-sustaining populations in South Dakota and Wyoming, with other populations—which may become self-sustaining in time—in Arizona, Colorado, Kansas, Montana, New Mexico, and Utah. Some black-footed ferrets from the captive-bred stock have been released in Mexico.

However, even in protected areas where prairie dogs are no longer trapped, shot, or poisoned, the future for the black-footed ferret looks uncertain. The main problem confronting the species is genetic. The entire surviving population of black-footed ferrets derives from a small handful of animals—the descendants of those taken into captivity in 1987—and as a result is dangerously inbred. Normally such inbreeding leads to poor reproductive success and a reduced chance of survival. It remains to be seen whether the newly restored populations, themselves bred from only a few dozen animals, will overcome their problems and increase to form a viable population. Even if they do, it is unlikely that they will ever again be widespread or numerous, simply because their prairie dog prey has disappeared from most of its former range.

The black-footed ferret *lives in prairie dog burrows. Its underground life and nocturnal habits explain why it is so little known. Yet despite its elusiveness, the ferret leaves tracks that are easily seen in snow, and the animal itself can sometimes be spotted at night by flashlight.*

Wolverine

Gulo gulo

The wolverine used to roam over much of Europe and North America. Today it is widely hunted for its fur and is increasingly rare. Its reputation as a bloodthirsty predator has also led to widespread persecution of the species.

Although it will eat all manner of things, the wolverine is a carnivore. It preys on small mammals, but often eats larger animals—such as deer—in the form of carrion. The decline of wolves and other large predators has reduced the availability of leftovers on which wolverines can feed. Human hunters deprive wolverines of even the scantiest scraps by removing their kills completely.

Under Pressure

Living at the edge of the Arctic, where food is scarce, a wolverine will kill in excess of its immediate need and store the surplus food for later. This apparent greed has given rise to its other common name: "glutton." Its lifestyle and skulking appearance have made the animal unpopular, and there are many folk tales among Arctic peoples about its cunning and bloodthirstiness. Reindeer herdsmen, for instance, fear that the wolverine will attack their animals, and trappers complain that wolverines steal bait and captured animals from their traps; the wolverine has many enemies eager to kill it on sight.

Wolverines have also been hunted for their fur. The long hairs tend not to freeze together in the intense cold of the Arctic, so the pelts are prized by native people for trimming the hoods of winter coats. The fur provides protection from the wind and does not become encrusted with ice from the wearer's frozen breath. Wolverines have been shot and trapped extensively across their northern range in Europe, North America, and Russia.

They used to be found much farther south than at present, even as far down as Germany in Europe and Arizona and New Mexico in the United States. Now they are extinct east of Montana; they had disappeared from the Midwest by the early 20th century. A few remain in California and Idaho. They are still widespread in Canada, although rare or extinct in the eastern provinces. British Columbia is a stronghold, with perhaps 4,000 to 5,000 animals. Little is known about numbers of wolverines in Russia and Siberia (where they occur east to Kamchatka), but they are believed to be still relatively numerous there. In northern Scandinavia wolverines have become rare, and most now occur in the remote mountains of Norway and Sweden. It is thought that there are only 40 left in Finland.

Naturally Scarce

Part of the problem lies in the fact that the wolverine is a naturally scarce animal. It ranges over vast areas and lives at low population densities. Often there is only one per 200 square miles (500 sq. km). This means that the animals rarely come across each other to breed. Fragmented populations become vulnerable to piecemeal extinction, dying out in one place after another with little chance of natural recolonization. Even a relatively low mortality rate can leave large gaps in the population. Mortality rates increase during periods of severe weather and food shortage.

Although wolverines have full legal protection in Scandinavia, they are still widely killed. Permits are even available to trap or kill the animals if they are believed to endanger domestic beasts such as reindeer.

Despite their reputation, wolverines are sensitive creatures and wary of humans. They are easily disturbed, and the isolated areas to which they have been driven are becoming increasingly accessible to motor vehicles. Road construction, tree-felling, and the building of cabins and houses threaten to invade the privacy of the few remaining wolverines.

The wolverine *resembles a small bear, but is actually the largest member of the weasel family. It is found in North America and northern Europe.*

DATA PANEL

Wolverine (glutton)

Gulo gulo

Family: Mustelidae

World population: Unknown, but low thousands

Distribution: Found widely across northern Canada and the U.S., northern Europe, and Russia

Habitat: Arctic and subarctic tundra and taiga

Size: Length head/body: 26–36 in (65–90 cm); tail: 5–10 in (13–25 cm); height at shoulder: 14–18 in (36–45 cm); females at least 10% smaller than males. Weight: 20–65 lb (9–30 kg)

Form: Largest member of weasel family; looks like a small bear. A low, thickset animal with short legs and large paws; tail thick and bushy; coat dark brown but paler on face, flanks, and base of tail. Sometimes pale all over

Diet: Mostly rodents (sometimes larger mammals); also fruit, berries, carrion, birds, and eggs; occasionally invertebrates

Breeding: Mates in summer, but development delayed until midwinter. Up to 4 young born (February–March), 1 litter per year. Life span up to 11 years in wild, 18 in captivity

Related endangered species: European mink (*Mustela lutreola*) EN; giant otter (*Pteronura brasiliensis*) EN; European otter (*Lutra lutra*) NT

Status: IUCN LC

Sea Otter

Enhydra lutris

Excessive hunting lead to the extermination of the sea otter from most of its range along north Pacific coasts. It recovered to about half its previous population levels through international protection, and is now stable.

The sea otter is one of the few mammals that uses tools: It employs a stone to smash open crabs, sea urchins, and mollusks caught on its shallow dives to the seabed. Intelligent animals, sea otters have learned to rip open sunken, discarded drink cans in which a small octopus may hide. Sea otters are important ecologically since they control the numbers of sea urchins, which eat a lot of growing kelp. Exposed coasts are protected against heavy wave action by the kelp beds. Where sea otter numbers have declined, urchins have increased and prevented proper growth of the floating kelp beds.

Sea otters are generally solitary animals, although they sometimes gather in groups. They are exclusively marine and usually fairly sedentary, but some occasionally go on long journeys, of about 100 miles (160 km) along the coast.

The sea otter lives in the cold waters of the north Pacific and spends a lot of time floating at the surface, grooming, or sleeping among the kelp beds. It is one of the smallest sea mammals and needs very effective insulation to reduce loss of body heat. Its fur is the densest known, with more than 600,000 hairs per square inch (93,000 per sq. cm)—twice the density of a fur seal's coat.

For centuries the thick pelt was highly valued, and the sea otter was ruthlessly hunted off the coasts of Kamchatka in Russia and in the eastern Pacific. Explorations by 18th-century navigators expanded the trade in skins, and colonization of Alaska by the Russians intensified the pressures on the species across the north Pacific. The skins became the world's most valuable fur, each pelt worth the equivalent of a seaman's wages for an

DATA PANEL

Sea otter

Enhydra lutris

Family: Mustelidae

World population: About 107,000 (2007)

Distribution: Coasts of California, eastern Russia (Kamchatka and Commander Islands). Successfully reintroduced to coasts of Alaska, Oregon, and Washington

Habitat: Rocky coasts and kelp beds

Size: Length head/body: 30–36 in (75–90 cm); tail: 11–13 in (28–32 cm); height at shoulder: 8–10 in (20–25 cm). Weight: 30–85 lb (14–40 kg)

Form: Dark-brown coat with a cream, blunt-looking head. The feet are completely webbed, the hind ones forming flippers

Diet: Crabs, shellfish, sea-urchins, fish, and other marine animals; about 13 lb (6 kg) daily

Breeding: Breeds all year round, but most births occur in early summer. Only 1 pup is born each year. Life span can exceed 20 years

Related endangered species: Giant otter (*Pteronura brasiliensis*) EN; European mink (*Mustela lutreola*) EN

Status: IUCN EN

entire year. Records show that over 750,000 sea otters were killed between 1750 and 1850, and that a single shipment of 17,000 skins was made in 1803.

Sea otters were easily hunted from kayaks; hunters chased the animals until they were too breathless to dive, then speared them. Each body would be skinned in the kayak and the next otter sought out. Living along the coast, and with no safety at sea, the otters could be hunted until every last one had been caught.

Success Story

Sea otters do not breed rapidly, so they became extinct over wide areas. In 1911 the Russians, Americans, and British (on behalf of Canada) agreed on total protection for the sea otter throughout the north Pacific. Gradually numbers have increased, and they are appearing again in many of their former

A sea otter *floats on its back. In such a position the animal can open a mollusk shell, crab, or sea-urchin by smashing it against a stone balanced on its chest.*

habitats. It was thought that sea otters were extinct on the California coast, but in 1938 a few were found. Numbers have grown to more than 3,000. In fact, fishermen now complain that there are too many. Animals have been transported to Washington state, Oregon, and Alaska, successfully repopulating those coasts; reintroductions to the Pribilof Islands off Alaska appear to have been less successful.

The sea otter, having been reduced to fewer than 1,000 animals in the whole North Pacific, has made a comeback. However, the otters still face a variety of threats—some of them natural, such as the risk of predation by killer whales. Others are man-made and include oil spills and other pollution.

Steller's Sea Lion

Eumetopias jubatus

Steller's sea lion was once considered a pest because of the quantities of fish it "stole" from humans. Now the situation has been reversed; Steller's sea lions are in decline because we eat too much of their food.

Although it is a widespread species, the number of Steller's sea lions has been declining since the 1980s, when there were about 290,000; today there thought to be 106,000–118,000. The western population, which extends across the Aleutian Islands to Japan, appears to be shrinking relatively slowly. The main losses seem to have occurred in the eastern population along the coasts of California, Oregon, British Columbia, and southern Alaska. Although the population there may still number about 39,000, it has declined by 83 percent in 30 years. If an animal population decreases that fast, action must be taken before it is too late.

Steller's sea lion used to be hunted for its meat, hide, and blubber, but commercial hunting stopped in the 1970s. About 400 are still killed each year for traditional uses by the indigenous peoples of Alaska (the skins make good canoe covers). Marine mammals in American waters have full legal protection, so large-scale killing of Steller's sea lions or disturbance of their breeding places should be prevented now and is unlikely to be the main cause of their decline. However, the animals are sometimes caught up in fishing nets. Around Vancouver Island licenses were issued to kill a few sea lions that were causing problems in fish-farming areas, and some illegal killing still goes on.

Oil spills and contamination of food by chemicals pose another threat to Steller's sea lion, as they do to many other species. Around Japan high levels of tributyl tin (TBT) have been reported in the bodies of sea lions. This is a poisonous substance found in the paint used to prevent barnacles from attaching to the hulls of boats.

Despite such hazards, the basic problem for Steller's sea lion seems to be a reduction in its food supply. The animals feed on fish,

DATA PANEL

Steller's sea lion (northern sea lion)

Eumetopias jubatus

Family: Otariidae

World population: Fewer than 120,000

Distribution: Edges of North Pacific and Bering Sea

Habitat: Coastal waters, offshore rocks and islands; also sea caves

Size: Length: male 9.2–10.5 ft (2.8–3.2 m); female 7.5–9.5 ft (2.3–2.9 m). Weight: male 1,240–2,470 lb (566–1,120 kg); female 580–770 lb (263–350 kg)

Form: Seal with coat of short, coarse hair; small ears; longer flippers than true seals. Males have manes

Diet: Fish, particularly pollock, salmon, herring, mackerel; sometimes squid and octopus

Breeding: Single pup born per year after 12-month gestation. Mature at about 4 years. Life span over 30 years in females, lower in males

Related endangered species: Guadeloupe fur seal (*Arctocephalus townsendii*) VU; Galápagos fur seal (*A. galapagoensis*) EN; Juan Fernandez fur seal (*A. philippii*) NT; northern fur seal (*Callorhinus ursinus*) VU; Hooker's sea lion (*Phocarctos hookeri*) VU

Status: IUCN EN

which they catch on or near the seabed, sometimes diving down to more than 1,200 feet (400 m) to get them. Trawlers harvest the same fish by dragging huge nets across the seabed. This competition for fish is a problem for the sea lions, especially around sea lion breeding colonies, where mother sea lions feed for up to three days at a time before returning to suckle their pups on the beaches.

Action against Fishing

Intensive commercial fishing has left fish stocks—especially walleye pollock—severely depleted. Trawlers were banned from fishing near sea lion breeding places throughout the 1990s. Exclusion zones were then extended to keep trawlers at least 22 miles (35 km) away from the colonies, and fishing restrictions were imposed all year round, not just in the breeding season. Fishermen were also made to spread their activities to reduce the pressure on fish stocks in certain areas. Around the Aleutian Islands, for instance, restrictions were placed

Steller's sea lion is in decline as a result of overfishing, but other factors may be at work too, including changes in sea currents.

on fishing for mackerel (another important food for the sea lions), and trawling for pollock was forbidden.

Such measures have come about partly as a result of lobbying by environmental campaigners. They must be taken seriously in order for us to prevent unpredictable and possibly irreversible damage to the North Pacific ecosystem and the extinction of Steller's sea lion.

Mediterranean Monk Seal

Monachus monachus

Although the monk seals of the Mediterranean are no longer hunted, they are extremely sensitive to disturbance of any kind. As many tourists know, undisturbed beaches in the Mediterranean are now few and far between.

The Greek philosopher and scientist Aristotle made the first scientific record of a seal in the 3rd century B.C. Since the Mediterranean monk is the only seal to inhabit the waters off southern Europe, there is little doubt that it was the species to which he referred. Ancient place names derived from the Greek word *phoca*, meaning seal, occur throughout Greece and Turkey, suggesting that the seals were once widespread in the region.

A few Mediterranean monk seals also live outside the Mediterranean. In fact, one of the largest remaining populations occurs in the tropical waters of Cap Blanc on the coast of Mauritania in northwestern Africa. One of the most remote and vulnerable populations lives around the Desertas Islands, a small group of rocky islets off Madeira. In 1989 that population contained just 10 individuals but has since increased to 20–23.

Environmental Disturbance

In more recent times the main hazard facing Mediterranean monk seal populations has come from environmental disturbance; the region's fishing and tourism industries are mostly to blame. Early records suggest that the seals used to pup on wide, sandy beaches, like those favored by their relative the Hawaiian monk seal. Yet today the same beaches are lined with hotels and visited by sunbathers and yachts. Consequently, the sensitive seals now rarely breed away from secluded coves surrounded by high cliffs, which are inaccessible to people. Most seals choose the even greater security of sea caves that can only be reached through underwater entrance tunnels.

Pregnant females are especially sensitive to disturbance, and even minor incidents can cause them to miscarry. Although they are physiologically capable of having one young every year, they rarely do so, and the overall reproduction rate is relatively low.

Another serious problem for the remaining scattered populations is competition with fishermen. The Mediterranean is one of the most intensively fished areas of water in the world. Humans and seals have similar tastes in seafood, including fish, octopus, and squid. Fishermen are none too willing to share their catch, and the seals make themselves very unpopular when they tear holes in the

DATA PANEL

Mediterranean monk seal

Monachus monachus

Family: Phocidae

World population: 350–450

Distribution: Scattered populations around the Mediterranean and on the Atlantic coast of Mauritania in northwestern Africa

Habitat: Sheltered subtropical coast; small beaches and sea caves

Size: Length: 7.5–9.2 ft (2.3–2.8 m). Weight: 550–660 lb (250–300 kg)

Form: Large seal with short, dark, variably patterned coat; pale patch on belly

Diet: Fish, octopus, and squid

Breeding: Single pup born May–November after gestation of 9–10 months; weaned at 6 weeks but stays with mother for 3 years; mature at 4 years. May live up to 23 years

Related endangered species: Hawaiian monk seal (*Monachus shauinslandi*) CR; Caribbean monk seal (*M. tropicalis*) EX

Status: IUCN CR

nets and make off with the contents. They regularly become entangled in the nets and, unable to return to the surface to breathe, drown in minutes.

It is largely as a result of centuries of hunting and habitat disturbance that the Mediterranean monk seal is now one of the world's rarest mammals. The sealing industry in the Mediterranean reached its peak in the 15th century; but even after hunting went into decline, the seal population continued to fall.

Still at Risk

The remaining Mediterranean monk seals are spread over a wide geographical area, and efforts to save them require determined international cooperation. The Greek population is now relatively secure; its breeding sites are protected within the Northern Sporades Marine Park. An intensive program of education, along with compensation for fishermen whose nets are damaged by seals, should mean that persecution is a thing of the past. However, even with

Mediterranean monk seals *basking on the rocks have been linked to the ancient Greek myth of the Sirens. The story goes that these deadly sea nymphs lured seamen onto the rocks with their beautiful singing.*

protection, populations are now so small that they are increasingly vulnerable to natural hazards. In 1978 a sea cave at Cap Blanc collapsed on a breeding colony, killing up to 50 seals. Such natural disasters could harm almost any population of large mammals, but for a population of fewer than 300 it was devastating. Until the Mediterranean monk seal population is large enough to survive such incidents, it will remain one of the world's most critically endangered species.

Florida Manatee

Trichechus manatus latirostris

Coastal development and the impact of fast speedboats threaten the Florida manatee. However, provided that its simple needs can be accommodated, there is no reason why these charming animals should not remain reasonably numerous.

There are two subspecies of the Caribbean or West Indian manatee. One, the Florida manatee, occurs in rivers and along nearby coasts. The other—the Antillean manatee—lives farther south in similar habitats.

Manatees usually occur in small family groups. They are slow-moving, sluggish animals that normally live on the edge of the sea and in sheltered lagoons. They will not tolerate water cooler than about 68°F (20°C) and often gather in warm places such as the areas where power stations discharge warm water into the sea—Cape Canaveral, Fort Myers, and Apollo Beach in Tampa Bay, for example. In summer they disperse widely along coasts and rivers.

Dangerous Waters

Manatees cannot come ashore since they have no hind limbs. When they breathe out, they become less buoyant and sink below the surface, where they paddle gently around seeking food. They can stay underwater for up to 30 minutes before they need to come up for air. For much of the time, however, they float around at the water surface looking like large logs, with only the tops of their backs visible. When floating, they are not easy to see, nor can they see far themselves.

In the coastal areas of Florida, where there are large numbers of water skiers, fast launches, and other boats, the waters have become unsafe for manatees. Many people have houses at the water's edge and use their boats for recreation, fishing, and transport. Collisions are frequent and often fatal for the manatees.

The number of boats and the disturbance caused by the huge increase in their use along the Florida coasts and lagoons have led to a steep decline in manatee numbers. It has been calculated that a reduction in manatee deaths of only 10 percent every year should be sufficient to allow the population to increase again. However, one obstacle to recovery is that manatees are very slow breeders, and even a small increase in adult mortality leads to a rapid decline in the population.

Apart from people (and some large sharks farther south than Florida), manatees have no natural predators. Nonetheless, for centuries people have killed them for their meat. Manatees are easy prey since they cannot swim fast or defend themselves effectively. Hunting is probably the main threat to manatees outside American waters; they also get tangled up and drown in commercial fishing nets.

Florida manatees are legally protected, and in certain places where the water is clear and they can be easily seen drifting around, they have become an important tourist attraction. Visitors and local people are paying more attention to this fascinating creature.

Setting Limits

People using boats are asked to avoid shallow water near the edges of rivers and lagoons (where there is plenty of aquatic vegetation) favored by the manatees. By imposing speed limits on small craft and providing separate channels for boats, conservationists are working toward a more secure future for the Florida manatee. With such measures in place there is no reason why the manatee should not survive in reasonable numbers.

The United States Fish and Wildlife Service has recently created a special manatee sanctuary at Three Sisters Springs in the Crystal River. More than 250 manatees spend the winter there because it is pleasantly warm. Disturbances from launches and boats had been forcing the animals out into colder waters, but this area is now off limits to visitors and boats between November and March.

The Florida manatee *population suffered in 1996, when over 155 were found dead. Agricultural chemicals may have been the cause, although natural toxins from algae in the water could have been responsible.*

DATA PANEL

Florida manatee

Trichechus manatus latirostris

Family: Trichechidae

World population: Florida subspecies more than 3,000; rest of the species probably 5,000–10,000

Distribution: Coast of the Gulf of Mexico north to Carolinas. Antillean subspecies extends around the Caribbean to southern Brazil

Habitat: Shallow, warm coastal waters; rivers and brackish water

Size: Length: 7–13 ft (2–4 m). Weight: up to 1,300 lb (590 kg); exceptionally up to 1.5 tons (1,500 kg)

Form: Large, sluggish animal; broad head and thick upper lip with spiky bristles; flippers at front but not at rear; tail flat, horizontal, and rounded

Diet: Wide assortment of floating and submerged water weeds, including water hyacinth and sea grass

Breeding: Single calf born May–September at intervals of 2–3 years after gestation of 11–13 months. Mature at 3–4 years. Life span up to 60 years

Related endangered species: Steller's sea cow (*Hydrodamalis gigas*) EX; African manatee (*Trichechus senegalensis*) VU; Amazon manatee (*T. inunguis*) VU; dugong (*Dugong dugon*) VU; Antillean manatee (*T. m. manatus*) VU

Status: IUCN VU

Tennessee
North Carolina
UNITED STATES South Carolina
Alabama Georgia
Florida
BAHAMAS

Przewalski's Wild Horse

Equus przewalskii

Excessive hunting, competition with domestic stock, and interbreeding with domestic horses have effectively caused the extinction of purebred herds of Przewalski's horse in the wild.

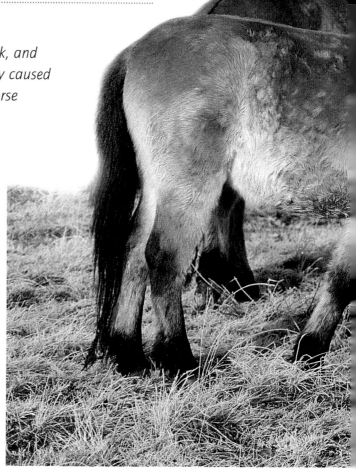

Przewalski's wild horse is named after the Russian general who discovered it while exploring Central Asia in 1879. It is, or was, the only species of true wild horse, but it is now extinct in its natural range. The horses used to live in large herds, each led by a dominant stallion, wandering the great grassy plains of Central Asia in considerable numbers. The animals would be on the move, feeding almost constantly, and always alert for danger. Although they were occasionally hunted for meat and hides, capture was not a significant threat while human populations remained low, and probably relatively few were killed. However, by the early 1900s hunting pressure had increased substantially, and the horse population began a steady decline in numbers.

The Przewalski's wild horse was given full legal protection in Mongolia in 1926. The legislation did not save the dwindling herds because the growing human population began to fence land for cultivation, excluding the horses from traditional feeding areas and vital places to drink. At the same time, the wild horses began to interbreed with domestic horses that were wandering freely in the same areas. The result was hybrid types and the steady dilution of the genetic integrity and typical features of the purebred wild horse herds. The last true Przewalski's wild horse was reported in 1968.

There now appear to be no Przewalski's horses surviving in the wild, but fortunately there are some in captivity. The horses were never domesticated but kept as a rarity in zoos. From a low point of just 13 animals numbers have been steadily increasing, and over 1,000 have been born in zoos. As a result of the small number of horses involved early on, inbreeding was a problem, leading to poor breeding success and low survival rates. However, zoos in Europe, North America, and the former Soviet Union collaborated constructively to manage a cooperative breeding program that aimed to share animals and to avoid matings between close relatives. About 200 horses are covered by this program, and purebred Przewalski's horses are now well established in captivity.

Reintroduction into the Wild

Many generations of captive breeding, artificial food, confinement in small enclosures, and living in mild climates away from Central Asia may all combine to

DATA PANEL

Przewalski's wild horse

Equus przewalskii

Family: Equidae

World population: Almost 2,000, including 325 free-ranging individuals in the wild

Distribution: Altai Mountains of Mongolia and (formerly) adjacent parts of China

Habitat: Dry, semidesert plain; steppe grassland

Size: Length head/body: 7 ft (2–2.1 m); tail: 36 in (90 cm); height at shoulder: 4 ft (1.2 m). Weight: 450–650 lb (200–300 kg)

Form: A stockily built pony with short neck and legs. The head is relatively heavy. The fur is sandy brown, much longer in winter, with a white area around the muzzle. Stiff, blackish hairs form an erect mane on the neck

Diet: Mainly grass, but also other small plants; shrubs and bark where they are available

Breeding: One foal born in April or May after 12-month gestation. Life span may exceed 25 years in captivity

Related endangered species: African wild ass (*Equus africanus*) CR; Asiatic wild ass (*E. hemionus*) EN; Grevy's zebra (*E. grevyi*) EN; mountain zebra (*E. zebra*) VU; quagga (*E. quagga*) EX

Status: IUCN CR

reduce the ability of the animals to survive in the extreme conditions of their native home. In 1989 an experiment was started at the Bukhara Breeding Center in Uzbekistan to find out whether horses bred for generations in zoos could actually survive the challenge of living wild in the semidesert conditions of Central Asia. A stallion and four mares were released into a huge fenced area and studied. The horses seemed to manage well; they bred successfully and did not suffer ill-effects from mixing with wild asses also present in the area. Efforts to restore Przewalski's horse to the wild have been successful in Mongolia. By 2008 there were 325 free-ranging horses there, all descended from captive-bred individuals. There are also plans to release captive-bred Przewalski's horses in China.

Przewalski's *is the only living species of truly wild horse. After becoming extinct in the wild it is now being reintroduced to its former range (see map) using animals bred in captivity.*

American Bison

Bison bison

Formerly America's most abundant large mammal and integral to the culture of native Americans, the bison was hunted to the brink of extinction during the development of North America. It is now numerous once more, and large herds live in protected areas and on ranches.

Plodding across the plains, bison look like pretty solid, sedate animals. However, they can swim, run fast—up to 30 mph (50 km/h)—and even jump over 3 feet (90 cm) into the air! They live in herds of up to several hundred animals, breaking up into smaller groups in winter. They make annual migrations to spread their feeding over a wide area. They also travel each day to drink. Today bison herds are limited in where they can roam because of towns, railways, and cattle fences. Mating takes place in July and August, when the largest numbers are gathered together. At this time the bulls make loud bellowing noises that can be heard 3 miles (5 km) away.

The bison was once abundant, with perhaps 60 million roaming across the American prairies. For many Native Americans bison were at the very center of their existence. The animals provided skins for homes and clothing; sinews were used as string or for sewing; the fur made cushions; and the meat was their main food. Paths made by the animals provided routes through dense vegetation and over rocky hills. The bison also caught the imagination of native American communities, figuring prominently in their folklore.

Slaughtered for Sport

As settlers pushed farther west, particularly during the 19th century, the plains were developed as farmland, and the bison were forced out of their ancestral range. Men like Buffalo Bill specialized in hunting the animals, particularly to feed the workers building the new railroads. The bison were also shot for sport, with hunters competing to see how many they could kill in a day. Once the railroads were running, it was also possible to export the meat and hides (bones too, for fertilizer) to distant markets. Out on the plains there was nowhere for the animals to hide, and they were ruthlessly pursued until in 1890 there were only a few hundred animals left alive.

DATA PANEL

American bison

Bison bison

Family: Bovidae

World population: 30,000 wild animals (and a further 500,000 in commercial populations)

Distribution: Midwestern U.S. and Canada

Habitat: Prairies and wooded areas

Size: Length: up to 12 ft (3.5 m); height at shoulder: up to 6.5 ft (1.9 m). Weight: 1,200–1,800 lb (500–800 kg); males up to 30% heavier than females

Form: Large, stocky animal with large hump over the shoulders; the head is held low. Dark-brown coat; forelegs, neck, and shoulders covered in long, shaggy hairs. Horns are present in both sexes

Diet: Mostly grass, also wild flowers, sedges, and shrubs such as willow, sagebrush, and birch. Active at all times, they eat over 1% of their weight per day and need water daily. In winter they scrape in the snow to get at lichens and mosses

Breeding: A single calf is born May–August after gestation of 9–10 months. It can run within 3 hours of birth and eats grass after the first week. Capable of breeding at 2–3 years. Life span up to 25 years

Related endangered species: European bison *(Bison bonasus)* VU

Status: IUCN NT

Fortunately, conservationists, led by William Hornaday, realized that one of America's national emblems was on the verge of extinction. Formed in 1905, the American Bison Society championed successful captive-breeding programs and herd management to ensure that the bison was saved from oblivion. Many have been released in areas from which they were lost long ago: Large numbers now exist in Alaska, where they were reintroduced in 1928. In many places bison now breed so successfully that they risk eating all the available food and starving during the winter. For this reason hunters are allowed to shoot small numbers each year to prevent the population getting too large. The meat is often in demand because it is less fatty than beef.

Bison are sometimes called buffalo, but they are more closely related to cattle and can breed with them. They also share similar diseases with cattle. True buffalo are quite different and are found in Africa.

Bison *are the largest animals on the American plains, living in herds numbering more than 100 individuals.*

EX
EW
CR
EN
VU
NT
LC
O

Arabian Oryx

Oryx leucoryx

In the vast deserts of the Middle East the oryx was hunted to extinction in the 1970s. It has now been reintroduced to the wild from captive herds bred in zoos.

Arabian oryx live in small herds, usually with fewer than 10 animals per group, which lessens the impact of their feeding on the sparse desert vegetation. They generally feed early in the day, then rest, and feed again before finding shade for the hottest part of the afternoon. The animals move around seasonally between feeding places and may use a total area of several thousand square miles in a year. They seem able to detect rain at a distance; they travel to the area affected to feed on the new growth of plants. Oryx prefer rocky or stony plains to soft sand and steep mountains.

Big-game hunters used to pursue oryx for trophies, and for generations the animals were hunted by men riding on camels. Although some escaped, many did not, and they were steadily eliminated from countries such as Syria, Egypt, and Israel. By the 1950s the increased availability of four-wheel drive vehicles, abundant fuel, automatic rifles, and oil-based local wealth combined to make hunting in Arab countries both more widespread and more efficient. Gunmen in vehicles hunted the animals to extinction. The last wild oryx were killed in the 1970s.

Rescue Remedy

Fortunately, several Arab countries had already made efforts to keep and breed the oryx in captivity. In 1962 international cooperation between zoos made it possible to assemble a

DATA PANEL

Arabian oryx (white oryx)

Oryx leucoryx

Family: Bovidae

World population: 1,100 in the wild (and a further 7,000–8,000 in captivity)

Distribution: Formerly in Egypt, Iraq, Israel, Syria, United Arab Emirates, and Yemen. Reintroduced to Jordan, Oman, and Saudi Arabia

Habitat: Rocky and stony plains in desert areas

Size: Length: 5–5.5 ft (1.5–1.6 m); height at shoulder: 32–41 in (81–104 cm). Weight: 140–155 lb (65–70 kg)

Form: A white antelope with black legs, each with a white band above the hoof. Horns (in both sexes) are straight, about 24 in (60 cm) long

Diet: Grasses and desert shrubs, from which they also get most of the water they need (although they may sometimes travel to a water hole)

Breeding: Births can occur in any month after 8-month gestation. The single calf stays with its mother for 4–5 months. Females are mature at about 3 years. Life span can be over 20 years

Related endangered species: Scimitar-horned oryx *(Oryx dammah)* EW

Status: IUCN EN

few animals in Phoenix, Arizona (where the climate is very similar to that of the native home of the Arabian oryx), from which to breed animals specifically for release back into the wild. This was the first such international project for any endangered or extinct species, and it has been highly successful. Oryx were released in Oman in 1982, and there were further releases in Israel and Saudi Arabia. In 2007 a new reintroduction program was started in Abu Dhabi. There are now about 1,100 Arabian oryx living wild, and many more in zoos and large natural enclosures.

Breeding large numbers of oryx from just a few individuals has inevitably led to genetic problems. Some of the more successful breeding males fathered a disproportionate number of the captive population in the early days. As a result of inbreeding, survival

Arabian oryx *are the palest species of oryx and are superbly adapted to life in the desert. Like other species of oryx, they are characterized by their long, upright horns. They have dark patches on their faces, legs, and at the lower end of the tail.*

rates were low; this problem has been recognized, and careful management of future breeding should ensure that it is overcome with time.

Oryx are now protected and have been adopted as an important symbol of the local culture in the countries to which they have been restored. It is unlikely that the species will die out a second time through carelessness, but the herds remain small, widely scattered, and vulnerable to natural disasters such as disease and drought.

Wild Yak

Bos grunniens

The ultimate "survival machine," the sturdy yak is in its element even in the harshest Himalayan winter conditions. However, it is not adapted to deal with the threats of hunting, habitat disturbance, and competition from its domesticated relatives.

Yaks are the eastern equivalent of the American bison, and they are among the hardiest mammals on earth. Between 2,000 and 3,000 years ago the yak's ancestors were successfully domesticated and used for milk, beef, and wool production. Domestic yaks were also used as pack and draft animals, and their dried dung served as fuel on the Tibetan plateau, which has no trees. Today the world population of domestic yaks is probably over 12 million. By contrast, wild yaks are now extremely rare: Recent estimates have put the population at just a few hundred animals.

An immensely hardy animal, the yak survives seemingly without difficulty on the hostile, high plateaus of the Himalayas, enduring winter conditions among the harshest on earth. Temperatures in this area can fall to as low as –15°F (–26°C). The yak uses heat generated by plant material fermenting in its intestines to help keep warm; adult yaks are also covered in thick, woolly hair. However, with such

adaptations to the extreme cold yaks are not so tolerant of warm temperatures. Herds that move to lower pastures to bear young in spring retreat as summer arrives, returning to altitudes of about 15,000 feet (4,550 m), where there is snow all year round.

Yaks are social animals, and most individuals will spend their lives as part of a herd. The largest herds are made up of females and young, with bachelor males forming smaller bands. There are obvious advantages to living in a group; formidable as fully grown yaks are, they still have at least one serious natural predator, namely, the Tibetan wolf.

Sure-Footed Climbers

The scarcity of good food in its habitat forces the yak to wander widely in search of grasses, lichens, and other low-growing alpine plants. Deep snow is hard to walk through, but the yaks save

DATA PANEL

Wild yak

Bos grunniens

Family: Bovidae

World population: Fewer than 15,000

Distribution: Tibetan plateau (northern Tibet); Kansu in northwestern China; eastern Kashmir in India

Habitat: Alpine tundra and steppe; spends summer above snow line

Size: Length: up to 10.6 ft (3.3 m); height at shoulder: up to 6.5 ft (2 m); females about 60% smaller than males. Weight: males 670–2,200 lb (300–1,000 kg); females lighter than males

Form: Massive ox with dense, brown-black woolly hair. High humped shoulders; low-slung head. Both sexes have curved horns

Diet: Grasses, herbs, and lichens

Breeding: Adults mate in winter; a single calf is born in the following fall. Life span up to 25 years

Related endangered species: American bison (*Bison bison*) NT

Status: IUCN VU

energy by walking in single file, stepping into the footprints of the animal in front. Each large cloven hoof is augmented with an enlarged dewclaw (a partly developed extra hoof), which gives a strong grip. Despite their bulk, the yaks are sure-footed climbers, able to hop from rock to rock to avoid the deepest snowdrifts. Only in the worst storms and blizzards do they come to a halt to wait out the weather, standing in small groups with their heads turned away from the driving wind and icy snow.

On the Brink of Extinction

The wild yak should surely be thriving in a habitat where no other species can match its power and suitability for the environment. It suffers from only moderate predation and has very little natural competition. However, as is so often the case, this magnificent example of natural design is being pushed to the brink of extinction by the actions of humans. Wild herds are hunted throughout much of their range; and as human settlements have expanded, yaks are finding themselves outcompeted by domestic herds or in some cases simply assimilated into them.

Wild and domestic yaks often interbreed. Consequently, the genetic purity of the wild type has been diluted, and the offspring are less able to cope with life in the wild.

The yak *is a massive, powerful creature with a voice to suit its stature. Its deep, grunting call has earned it a scientific name that translates literally as "grunting ox."*

Ryukyu Flying Fox

Pteropus dasymallus

The Ryukyu flying fox is typical of many fruit bats living on islands; it faces a range of threats, and already one subspecies seems to be extinct.

There are five local varieties of the Ryukyu flying fox, which vary in size and color. They each live on different islands; and because their habitats are mostly small, the animals have probably never been very numerous.

The flying foxes are not foxes at all, but large fruit-eating bats. They live in the warmer regions of Asia and on islands in the Pacific and Indian Oceans. Like other flying foxes, they form colonies, hanging like furled umbrellas, spaced out along the bare branches of trees. Sometimes the colonies are large and conspicuous. Their habit of hanging out in the open makes the bats vulnerable to the slightest disturbance and to being shot or captured.

Capture is a common problem for all the larger fruit bats, since they are meaty and good to eat. Large numbers have been routinely collected for food, often by plundering the nursery colonies where the young bats are reared. Such disturbance results in the loss or abandonment of many youngsters. Like other bats, if the young fall to the ground before they can fly properly, they are generally unable to get airborne again. Often they are killed by dogs, land crabs, and even armies of ants. Bats also produce only one young a year, so replacement of losses is a slow process.

Ecological Eating

Fruit bats feed mainly on soft fruit borne by trees in the forest. They often just squeeze the fruit in their mouths and swallow only the juice, spitting out (or dropping) most of the pips and pulp at some distance from the tree. Any swallowed pips or seeds pass undamaged through the digestive tract and are discarded with the feces, often miles from where the fruit was collected. This is an important mechanism for dispersing the seeds of forest trees. Many fruit bats, including the Ryukyu flying fox, also feed on flowers at certain times of the year and help pollinate them, thus performing another essential ecological role. Consequently, the preservation of fruit bat populations is needed for the continued survival of a sustainable forest ecosystem.

DATA PANEL

Ryukyu flying fox

Pteropus dasymallus

Family: Pteropodidae

World population: Probably low thousands

Distribution: Ryukyu (Nansei) Islands, Japan

Habitat: Forest, fruit trees

Size: Length: 8 in (22 cm); wingspan: over 3 ft (1 m). Weight: 1 lb (400–450 g)

Form: Large fruit bat with typical "foxy" face and big eyes. Varies in color from pale brown to black, sometimes with pale collar or chest

Diet: Variety of fruit, especially figs; also flowers, insects, and leaves

Breeding: One young born per year. Life span unknown but could be 20 years

Related endangered species: Rodrigues flying fox *(Pteropus rodricensis)* CR. The IUCN lists 48 other species of *Pteropus* among the threatened mammals, including 3 others that are Critically Endangered

Status: IUCN NT

A Fragile Future

The conservation of flying foxes and other fruit bats is essential, yet many species are threatened and fast disappearing. For example, numbers of the Taiwanese subspecies of the Ryukyu flying fox have declined sharply as a result of poor enforcement of protection laws. Recent surveys have failed to find any individuals, and this flying fox may already be extinct. Elsewhere, other subspecies of the Ryukyu flying fox are threatened by loss of habitat in which to roost and feed as trees are removed for the timber industry, fuel, and to create farmland.

In the past hunters have killed large numbers of flying foxes, reducing the population drastically. In some places the bats also sustain losses through flying

The Ryukyu flying fox, like other species of flying fox, has a doglike face and large ears. Flying foxes navigate using their eyesight and sense of smell to locate the fruit and flowers on which they feed at night.

into overhead electricity and telephone wires. Contact with the wires can result in electrocution, strangulation, or broken wings.

The Japanese government has given the Ryukyu flying fox legal protection. However, it has not created any protected areas in which the bats can live undisturbed. Although the flying fox is reported to be numerous on a couple of the islands around Japan, forest removal is still badly affecting the Ryukyu group.

Categories of Threat

The status categories that appear in the data panel for each species throughout this book are based on those published by the International Union for the Conservation of Nature (IUCN). They provide a useful guide to the current status of the species in the wild, and governments throughout the world use them when assessing conservation priorities and in policy-making. However, they do not provide automatic legal protection for the species.

Animals are placed in the appropriate category after scientific research. More species are being added all the time, and animals can be moved from one category to another as their circumstances change.

Extinct (EX)

A group of animals is classified as EX when there is no reasonable doubt that the last individual has died.

Extinct in the Wild (EW)

Animals in this category are known to survive only in captivity or as a population established artificially by introduction somewhere well outside its former range. A species is categorized as EW when exhaustive surveys throughout the areas where it used to occur consistently fail to record a single individual. It is important that such searches be carried out over all of the available habitat and during a season or time of day when the animals should be present.

Critically Endangered (CR)

The category CR includes animals facing an extremely high risk of extinction in the wild in the immediate future. It includes any of the following:
- Any species with fewer than 50 individuals, even if the population is stable.
- Any species with fewer than 250 individuals if the population is declining, badly fragmented, or all in one vulnerable group.
- Animals from larger populations that have declined by 80 percent within 10 years (or are predicted to do so) or three generations, whichever is the longer.

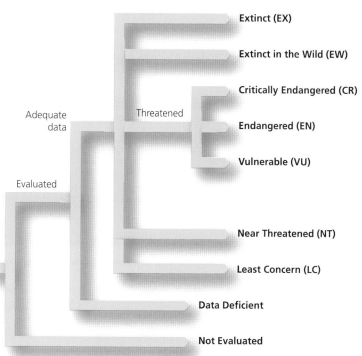

Adequate data

Threatened

Evaluated

- Extinct (EX)
- Extinct in the Wild (EW)
- Critically Endangered (CR)
- Endangered (EN)
- Vulnerable (VU)
- Near Threatened (NT)
- Least Concern (LC)
- Data Deficient
- Not Evaluated

The IUCN categories
of threat. The system displayed has operated for new and reviewed assessments since January 2001.

• Species living in a very small area—defined as under 39 square miles (100 sq. km).

Endangered (EN)

A species is EN when it is not CR but is nevertheless facing a very high risk of extinction in the wild in the near future. It includes any of the following:

• A species with fewer than 250 individuals remaining, even if the population is stable.

• Any species with fewer than 2,500 individuals if the population is declining, badly fragmented, or all in one vulnerable subpopulation.

• A species whose population is known or expected to decline by 50 percent within 10 years or three generations, whichever is the longer.

• A species whose range is under 1,900 square miles (5,000 sq. km), and whose range, numbers, or population levels are declining, fragmented, or fluctuating wildly.

• Species for which there is a more than 20 percent likelihood of extinction in the next 20 years or five generations, whichever is the longer.

Vulnerable (VU)

A species is VU when it is not CR or EN but is facing a high risk of extinction in the wild in the medium-term future. It includes any of the following:

• A species with fewer than 1,000 mature individuals remaining, even if the population is stable.

• Any species with fewer than 10,000 individuals if the population is declining, badly fragmented, or all in one vulnerable subpopulation.

• A species whose population is known, believed, or expected to decline by 20 percent within 10 years or

The American bison was almost wiped out by overhunting. With the population reduced to just 800 by about 1875 (below), intensive conservation measures saved the species from extinction. These bison (left) have radio-transmitter collars that allow scientists to track their movements.

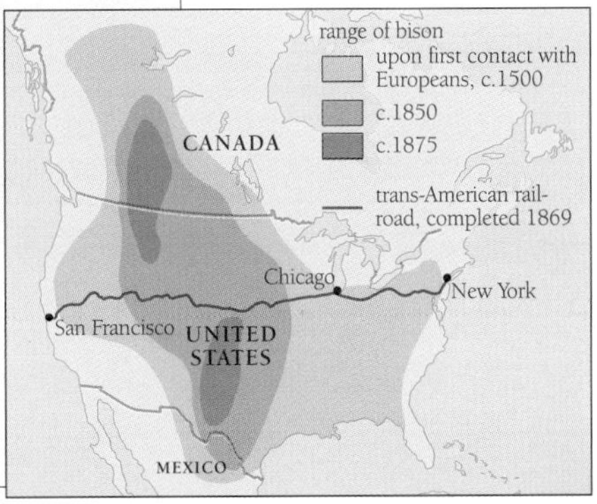

range of bison
upon first contact with Europeans, c.1500
c.1850
c.1875
trans-American railroad, completed 1869

CANADA

Chicago
New York
San Francisco UNITED STATES

MEXICO

three generations, whichever is the longer.
• A species whose range is less than 772 square miles (20,000 sq. km), and whose range, numbers, or population structure are declining, fragmented, or fluctuating wildly.
• Species for which there is a more than 10 percent likelihood of extinction in the next 100 years.

Near Threatened/Least Concern (since 2001)

In January 2001 the classification of lower-risk species was changed. Near Threatened (NT) and Least Concern (LC) were introduced as separate categories. They replaced the previous Lower Risk (LR) category with its subdivisions of Conservation Dependent (LRcd), Near Threatened (LRnt), and Least Concern (LRlc). From January 2001 all new assessments and reassessments must adopt NT or LC if relevant. But the older categories still apply to many animals until they are reassessed, and will also be found in this book.
• Near Threatened (NT)
Animals that do not qualify for CR, EN, or VU categories now but are close to qualifying or are likely to qualify for a threatened category in the future.
• Least Concern (LC)
Animals that have been evaluated and do not qualify for CR, EN, VU, or NT categories.

Lower Risk (before 2001)

• Conservation Dependent (LRcd)
Animals whose survival depends on an existing conservation program
• Near Threatened (LRnt)
Animals for which there is no conservation program but that are close to qualifying for VU category.
• Least Concern (LRlc)

By monitoring *populations of threatened animals like this American rosy boa, biologists help keep the IUCN Red List up to date.*

Their secretive habits *ensure that tiger populations are difficult to assess accurately. However, it is known that their numbers are declining.*

Species that are not conservation dependent or near threatened.

Data Deficient (DD)

A species or population is DD when there is not enough information on abundance and distribution to assess the risk of extinction. In some cases, when the species is thought to live only in a small area, or a considerable period of time has passed since the species was last recorded, it may be placed in a threatened category as a precaution.

Not Evaluated (NE)

Such animals have not yet been assessed.

Note: a colored panel in each entry in this book indicates the current level of threat to the species. The two new categories (NT and LC) and two of the earlier Lower Risk categories (LRcd and LRnt) are included within the band LR; the old LRlc is included along with Data Deficient (DD) and Not Evaluated (NE) under "Other," abbreviated to "O."

CITES *lists animals in the major groups in three Appendices, depending on the level of threat posed by international trade.*

	Appendix I	Appendix II	Appendix III
Mammals	277 species 16 subspecies 14 populations	295 species 12 subspecies 12 populations	45 species 8 subspecies
Birds	152 species 11 subspecies 2 populations	1,268 species 6 subspecies 1 populations	35 species
Reptiles	75 species 5 subspecies 6 populations	527 species 4 subspecies 4 populations	55 species
Amphibians	16 species	98 species	
Fish	15 species	71 species	
Invertebrates	62 species 4 subspecies	2,100 species 1 subspecies	17 species

CITES APPENDICES

Appendix I lists the most endangered of traded species, namely those that are threatened with extinction and will be harmed by continued trade. These species are usually protected in their native countries and can only be imported or exported with a special permit. Permits are required to cover the whole transaction—both exporter and importer must prove that there is a compelling scientific justification for moving the animal from one country to another. This includes transferring animals between zoos for breeding purposes. Permits are only issued when it can be proved that the animal was legally acquired and that the remaining population will not be harmed by the loss.

Appendix II includes species that are not currently threatened with extinction, but that could easily become so if trade is not carefully controlled. Some common animals are listed here if they resemble endangered species so closely that criminals could try to sell the rare species pretending they were a similar common one. Permits are required to export such animals, with requirements similar to those Appendix I species.

Appendix III species are those that are at risk or protected in at least one country. Other nations may be allowed to trade in animals or products, but they may need to prove that they come from safe populations.

CITES designations are not always the same for every country. In some cases individual countries can apply for special permission to trade in a listed species. For example, they might have a safe population of an animal that is very rare elsewhere. Some African countries periodically apply for permission to export large quantities of elephant tusks that have been in storage for years, or that are the product of a legal cull of elephants. This is controversial because it creates an opportunity for criminals to dispose of black market ivory by passing it off as coming from one of those countries where elephant products are allowed to be exported. If you look up the African elephant, you will see that it is listed as CITES I, II, and III, depending on the country location of the different populations.

Organizations

The human race is undoubtedly nature's worst enemy, but we can also help limit the damage caused by the rapid increase in our numbers and activities. There have always been people eager to protect the world's beautiful places and to preserve its most special animals, but it is only quite recently that the conservation message has begun to have a real effect on everyday life, government policy, industry, and agriculture.

Early conservationists were concerned with preserving nature for the benefit of people. They acted with an instinctive sense of what was good for nature and people, arguing for the preservation of wilderness and animals in the same way as others argued for the conservation of historic buildings or gardens. The study of ecology and environmental science did not really take off until the mid-20th century, and it took a long time for the true scale of our effect in the natural world to become apparent. Today the conservation of wildlife is based on far greater scientific understanding, but the situation has become much more complex and urgent in the face of human development.

By the mid-20th century extinction was becoming an immediate threat. Animals such as the passenger pigeon, quagga, and thylacine had disappeared despite last-minute attempts to save them. More and more species were discovered to be at risk, and species-focused conservation groups began to appear. In the early days there was little that any of these organizations could do but campaign against direct killing. Later they became a kind of conservation emergency service—rushing to the aid of seriously threatened animals in an attempt to save the species. But as time went on, broader environmental issues began to receive the urgent attention they needed. Research showed time and time again that saving species almost always comes down to addressing the

Conservation *organizations range from government departments in charge of national parks, such as Yellowstone National Park (right), the oldest in the United States, to local initiatives set up to protect endangered birds. Here (above) a man in Peru climbs a tree to check on the nest of a harpy eagle discovered near his village.*

problem of habitat loss. The world is short of space, and ensuring that there is enough for all the species is very difficult.

Conservation is not just about animals and plants, nor even the protection of whole ecological systems. Conservation issues are so broad that they touch almost every aspect of our lives, and successful measures often depend on the expertise of biologists, ecologists, economists, diplomats, lawyers, social scientists, and businesspeople. Conservation is all about cooperation and teamwork. Often it is also about helping people benefit from taking care of their wildlife. The organizations involved vary from small groups of a few dozen enthusiasts in local communities to vast, multinational operations.

THE IUCN

With so much activity based in different countries, it is important to have a worldwide overview, some way of coordinating what goes on in different parts of the planet. That is the role of the International Union for the Conservation of Nature (IUCN), also referred to as the World Conservation Union. It began life as the International Union for the Preservation of Nature in 1948, becoming the IUCN in 1956. It is relatively new compared to the Sierra Club, Flora & Fauna International, and the Royal Society for the Protection of Birds. It was remarkable in that its founder members included governments, government agencies, and nongovernmental organizations. In the

years following the appalling destruction of World War II, the IUCN was born out of a desire to draw a line under the horrors of the past and to act together to safeguard the future.

The mission of the IUCN is to influence, encourage, and assist societies throughout the world to conserve the diversity of nature and natural systems. It seeks to ensure that the use of natural resources is fair and ecologically sustainable. Based in Switzerland, the IUCN has over 1,000 permanent staff and the help of 11,000 volunteer experts from about 180 countries. The work of the IUCN is split into six commissions, which deal with protected areas, policy-making, ecosystem management, education, environmental law, and species survival. The Species Survival Commission (SSC) has almost 7,000 members, all experts in the study of plants and animals. Within the SSC there are Specialist Groups concerned with the conservation of different types of animals, from cats to flamingos, deer, ducks, bats, and crocodiles. Some particularly well-studied animals, such as the African elephant and the polar bear, have their own specialist groups.

Perhaps the best-known role of the IUCN SSC is in the production of the Red Data Books, or Red Lists. First published in 1966, the books were designed to be easily updated, with details of each species on a different page that could be removed and replaced as new information came to light.

By 2010 the Red Lists include information on about 45,000 types of animal, of which almost 10,000 are threatened with extinction. Gathering this amount of information together is a

The IUCN Red Lists *of threatened species are published online and can be accessed at: http://www. iucnredlist.org*

huge task, but it provides an invaluable conservation resource. The Red Lists are continually updated and are now available on the World Wide Web. The Red Lists are the basis for the categories of threat used in this book.

CITES

CITES is the Convention on International Trade in Endangered Species of Wild Fauna and Flora (also known as the Washington Convention, since it first came into force after an international meeting in Washington D.C. in 1973). Currently 175 nations have agreed to implement the CITES regulations. Exceptions to the convention include Iraq and North Korea, which, for the time being at least, have few trading links with the rest of the world. Trading in animals and their body parts has been a major factor in the decline of some of the world's rarest species. The IUCN categories draw attention to the status of rare species, but they do not confer any legal protection. That is done through national laws.

Conventions serve as international laws. In the case of CITES, lists (called Appendices) are agreed on internationally and reviewed every few years. The Appendices list the species that are threatened by international trade. Animals are assigned to Appendix I when all trade is forbidden. Any specimens of these species, alive or dead (or skins, feathers, etc.), will be confiscated by customs at international borders, seaports, or airports. Appendix II species can be traded internationally, but only under strict controls. Wildlife trade is often valuable in the rural economy, and this raises difficult questions about the relative importance of animals and people. Nevertheless, traders who ignore CITES rules risk heavy fines or imprisonment. Some rare species—even those with the highest IUCN categories (many bats and frogs, for example)—may have no CITES protection simply because they have no commercial value. Trade is then not really a threat.

The Greenpeace ship, *seen here in Antarctica, travels to areas of conservation concern and helps draw worldwide media attention to environmental issues.*

WILDLIFE CONSERVATION ORGANIZATIONS

BirdLife International
BirdLife International is a partnership of 60 organizations working in more than 100 countries. Most partners are national nongovernmental conservation groups such as the Canadian Nature Federation. Others include large bird charities such as the Royal Society for the Protection of Birds in Britain. By working together within BirdLife International, even small organizations can be effective globally as well as on a local scale. BirdLife International is a member of the IUCN.
Web site: http://www.birdlife.org

Conservation International (CI)
Founded in 1987, Conservation International works closely with the IUCN and has a similar multinational approach. CI offers help in the world's most threatened biodiversity hot spots.
Web site: http://conservation.org

Durrell Wildlife Conservation Trust (DWCT)
Another IUCN member, the Durrell Wildlife Conservation Trust was founded by the British naturalist and author Gerald Durrell in 1963. The trust is based at Durrell's world-famous zoo on Jersey in the Channel Islands. Jersey was the world's first zoo dedicated solely to the conservation of endangered species. Breeding programs at the zoo have helped stabilize populations of some of the world's most endangered animals. The trust trains conservationists from many countries and works to secure areas of natural habitat to which animals can be returned. Jersey Zoo and the DWCT were instrumental in saving numerous species from extinction, including the pink pigeon, Mauritius kestrel, Waldrapp ibis, St. Lucia parrot, and the Telfair's skink and other reptiles.
Web site: http://durrell.org

Fauna & Flora International (FFI)
Founded in 1903, this organization has had various name changes. It began life as a society for protecting large mammals, but has broadened its scope. It was involved in saving the Arabian oryx from extinction.
Web site: http://www.fauna-flora.org

National Audubon Society
John James Audubon was an American naturalist and wildlife artist who died in 1851, 35 years before the society that bears his name was founded. The first Audubon Society was established by George Bird Grinnell in protest against the appalling overkill of birds for meat, feathers, and sport. By the end of the 19th century there were Audubon Societies in 15 states, and they later became part of the National Audubon Society, which funds scientific research programs, publishes

WILDLIFE CONSERVATION ORGANIZATIONS

magazines and journals, manages wildlife sanctuaries, and advises state and federal governments on conservation issues. Web site: http://www.audubon.org

Pressure Groups
Friends of the Earth, founded in Britain in 1969, and Greenpeace, founded in 1971 in British Columbia, were the first environmental pressure groups to become internationally recognized. Greenpeace became known for "direct, nonviolent actions," which drew attention to major conservation issues. (For example, campaigners steered boats between the harpoon guns of whalers and their prey.)

The organizations offer advice to governments and corporations, and help those that seek to protect the environment, while continuing to name, shame, and campaign against those who do not.

Royal Society for the Protection of Birds
This organization was founded in the 1890s to campaign against the slaughter of birds to supply feathers for the fashion trade. It now has a wider role and has become Britain's premier wildlife conservation organization, with over a million members. It is involved in international activities, particularly in the protection of birds that migrate to Britain. Web site: http://www.rspb.org.uk

The Sierra Club
The Sierra Club was started in 1892 by John Muir and is still going strong. Muir, a Scotsman by birth, is often thought of as the founder of the conservation movement, especially in the United States, where he campaigned for the preservation of wilderness. It was through his efforts that the first national parks, including Yosemite,

Sequoia, and Mount Rainier, were established. Today the Sierra Club remains dedicated to the preservation of wild places for the benefit of wildlife and the enjoyment of people. Web site: http://www.sierraclub.org

World Wide Fund for Nature (WWF)
The World Wide Fund for Nature, formerly the World Wildlife Fund, was born in 1961. It was a joint venture between the IUCN, several existing conservation organizations, and a number of successful businesspeople. Unlike many charities, WWF was big, well-funded, and high profile from the beginning. Its familiar giant panda emblem ranks alongside those of the Red Cross, Mercedes Benz, or Coca-Cola in terms of instant international recognition. Web site: http://www.wwf.org

GLOSSARY

adaptation Features of an animal that adjust it to its environment; may be produced by evolution—e.g., camouflage coloration

adaptive radiation Where a group of closely related animals (e.g., members of a family) have evolved differences from each other so that they can survive in different niches

alpine Living in mountainous areas, usually over 5,000 feet (1,500 m)

anterior The front part of an animal

arboreal Living in trees

baleen Horny substance commonly known as whalebone and growing as plates in the mouth of certain whales; used as a fringelike sieve for extracting plankton from seawater

biodiversity The variety of species and the variation within them

biome A major world landscape characterized by having similar plants and animals living in it, e.g., desert, rain forest, forest

blowhole The nostril opening on the head of a whale through which it breathes

browsing Feeding on the leaves of trees and shrubs

canine tooth A sharp stabbing tooth usually longer than the rest

carnivore An animal that eats other animals

carrion Rotting flesh of dead animals

cloaca Cavity in the pelvic region into which the alimentary canal, genital, and urinary ducts open

diurnal Active during the day

DNA (deoxyribonucleic acid) The substance that makes up the main part of the chromosomes of all living things; contains the genetic code that is handed down from generation to generation

domestication Process of taming and breeding animals to provide help and useful products for humans

dormancy A state in which—as a result of hormone action—growth is suspended and metabolic activity is reduced to a minimum

dorsal Relating to the back or spinal part of the body; usually the upper surface

echolocation The process of perception based on reaction to the pattern of reflected sound waves (echos); occurs in bats

ecology The study of plants and animals in relation to one another and to their surroundings

ecosystem A whole system in which plants, animals, and their environment interact

edentate Toothless; also any animals of the order Edentata, which includes anteaters, sloths, and armadillos

endemic Found only in one geographical area, nowhere else

estivation Inactivity or greatly decreased activity during hot weather

eutrophication an increase in the nutrient chemicals (nitrate, phosphate, etc.) in water, sometimes occurring naturally and sometimes caused by human activities, e.g., by the release of sewage or agricultural fertilizers

extinction Process of dying out at the end of which the very last individual dies, and the species is lost forever

feral Domestic animals that have gone wild and live independently of people

fluke Either of the two lobes of the tail of a whale or related animal; also a type of flatworm, usually parasitic

gene The basic unit of heredity, enabling one generation to pass on characteristics to its offspring

gestation The period of pregnancy in mammals, between fertilization of the egg and birth of the baby

harem A group of females living in the same territory and consorting with a single male

herbivore An animal that eats plants (grazers and browsers are herbivores)

hibernation Becoming inactive in winter, with lowered body temperature to save energy. Hibernation takes place in a special nest or den called a hibernaculum

homeotherm An animal that can maintain a high and constant body temperature by means of internal processes; also called "warm-blooded"

inbreeding Breeding among closely related animals (e.g., cousins), leading to weakened genetic composition and reduced survival rates

insectivore Animal that feeds on insects. Also used as a group name for hedgehogs, shrews, moles, etc.

keratin Tough, fibrous material that forms hair, feathers, nails, and protective plates on the skin of vertebrate animals

krill Planktonic shrimps

mammal Any animal of the class Mammalia—warm-blooded vertebrate having mammary glands in the female that produce milk with which it nurses its young. The class includes bats, primates, rodents, and whales

matriarch Senior female member of a social group

metabolic rate The rate at which chemical activities occur within animals, including the exchange of gasses in respiration and the liberation of energy from food

monotreme Egg-laying mammal, e.g., platypus

olfaction Sense of smell

omnivore An animal that eats a wide range of both animal and vegetable food

parasite An animal or plant that lives on or within the body of another (the host) from which it obtains nourishment. The host is often harmed by the association

pelagic Living in the upper waters of the open sea or large lakes

pheromone Scent produced by animals to enable others to find and recognize them

placenta The structure that links an embryo to its mother during pregnancy, allowing exchange of chemicals between them

posterior The hind end or behind another structure

prehensile Capable of grasping

primates A group of mammals that includes monkeys, apes, and ourselves

quadruped Any animal that walks on four legs

ruminant Animals that eat vegetation and later bring it back from the stomach to chew again ("chewing the cud") to assist its digestion by microbes in the stomach

underfur Fine hairs forming a dense, woolly mass close to the skin and underneath the outer coat of stiff hairs in mammals

ungulate One of a large group of hoofed animals such as pigs, deer, cattle, and horses; mostly herbivores

uterus Womb in which embryos of mammals develop

vertebrate Animal with a backbone (e.g., fish, mammal, reptile), usually with skeleton made of bones, but sometimes softer cartilage

viviparous (of most mammals and a few other vertebrates) Giving birth to active young rather than laying eggs

FURTHER RESEARCH

Books

Mammals
Macdonald, David, *The New Encyclopedia of Mammals,* Oxford University Press, Oxford, U.K., 2009

Payne, Roger, *Among Whales*, Bantam Press, U.S., 1996

Reeves, R. R., and Leatherwood, S., *The Sierra Club Handbook of Whales and Dolphins of the World*, Sierra Club, U.S., 1983

Sherrow, Victoria, and Cohen, Sandee, *Endangered Mammals of North America*, Twenty-First Century Books, U.S., 1995

Whitaker, J. O., Audubon Society
Field Guide to North American Mammals, Alfred A. Knopf, New York, U.S., 1996

Wilson, Don E., Mittermeier, Russell A., *Handbook of Mammals of the World Vol 1,* Lynx Edicions, Barcelona, Spain, 2009

Birds
Attenborough, David, *The Life of Birds,* BBC Books, London, U.K., 1998

BirdLife International, *Threatened Birds of the World*, Lynx Edicions, Barcelona, Spain and BirdLife International, Cambridge, U.K., 2000

del Hoyo, J., Elliott, A., and Sargatal, J., eds., *Handbook of Birds of the World Vols 1 to 15,* Lynx Edicions, Barcelona, Spain, 1992–2010

Dunn, Jon, and Alderfer, Jonathan K., *National Geographic Field Guide to the Birds of North America,* National Geographic Society, Washington D.C., United States, 2006.

Stattersfield, A., Crosby, M., Long, A., and Wege, D., eds., *Endemic Bird Areas of the World: Priorities for Biodiversity Conservation,* BirdLife International, Cambridge, U.K., 1998

Fish
Buttfield, Helen, *The Secret Lives of Fishes*, Abrams, U.S., 2000

Dawes, John, and Campbell, Andrew, eds., *The New Encyclopedia of Aquatic Life, Facts On File*, New York, U.S., 2004

Reptiles and Amphibians
Corbett, Keith, *Conservation of European Reptiles and Amphibians,* Christopher Helm, London, U.K., 1989

Corton, Misty, *Leopard and Other South African Tortoises,* Carapace Press, London, U.K., 2000

Hofrichter, Robert, *Amphibians: The World of Frogs, Toads, Salamanders, and Newts*, Firefly Books, Canada, 2000

Murphy, J. B., Adler, K., and Collins, J. T. (eds.), *Captive Management and Conservation of Reptiles and Amphibians*, Society for the Study of Amphibians and Reptiles, Ithaca, New York, 1994

Stafford, Peter, *Snakes*, Natural History Museum, London, U.K., 2000

Insects
Eaton, Eric R. and Kaufman, Kenn. *Kaufman Field Guide to Insects of North America*, Houghton Mifflin, New York, U.S., 2007

Pyle, Robert Michael, National Audubon Society *Field Guide to North American Butterflies*, Pyle, Robert Michael, A. Knopf, New York, U.S., 1995

General
Allaby, Michael, *A Dictionary of Ecology*, Oxford University Press, New York, U.S., 2010

Douglas, Dougal, and others, *Atlas of Life on Earth*, Barnes & Noble, New York, U.S., 2001

Web sites
http://www.nature.nps.gov/ U.S. National Park Service wildlife site

http://www.ummz.lsa.umich-edu/
umich.edu/ University of Michigan Museum of Zoology animal diversity web. Search for pictures and information about animals by class, family, and common name

http://www.cites.org/ CITES and IUCN listings. Search for animals by order, family, genus, species, or common name. Location by country and explanation of reasons for listings

http://www.cmc-ocean.org Facts, figures, and quizzes about marine life

www.darwinfoundation.org/ Charles Darwin Research Center

http://www.fws.gov.endangered Information about endangered animals and plants from the U.S. Fish and Wildlife Service, the organization in charge of 94 million acres of wildlife refuges

http://www.endangeredspecie.com
Information, links, books, and publications about rare and endangered species. Also includes information about conservation efforts and organizations

http://forests.org/ Includes forest conservation answers to queries

http://www.iucn.org Details of species, IUCN listings, and IUCN publications. Link to online Red Lists of threatened species at: www.iucnredlist.org

http://www.panda.org World Wide Fund for Nature (WWF). Newsroom, press releases, government reports, campaigns. Themed photogallery

http://wdcs.org/ Whale and Dolphin Conservation Society site. News, projects, and campaigns. Sightings database

INDEX

Words and page numbers in **bold type** indicate main references to the various topics.